Teaching Disabled Children in Physical Education

This book examines the role that research plays in pedagogical practices when teaching disabled children and young people in physical education classes. It scrutinises the practices that are commonly used by teachers and coaches, and advocated by academics, and explores the evidence base that supports them.

This book covers disability broadly, including a focus on autism, learning difficulties, and visual impairment. It offers guidance to practitioners by explaining what is (or is not) available to support commonly suggested pedagogical practices, paying particular attention to research highlighting the voices of disabled persons and feelings associated with inclusion (that is, belonging, acceptance, and value), and whether these practices can help disabled students enjoy these subjective experiences.

Bringing together the very latest research with an assessment of current – and future – pedagogical practices, this concise and insightful book is invaluable reading for all pre-service and in-service teachers or coaches with an interest in physical education, disability, or special educational needs, as well as any advanced student or researcher working in these areas.

Anthony J. Maher is Director of Research and Professor of Special Educational Needs, Disability and Inclusion in the Carnegie School of Education at Leeds Beckett University, UK. Anthony's research, consultancy, and teaching expertise relate to centring the experiences and amplifying the voices of pupils with special educational needs and disabilities (SEND). This is part of his commitment to trying to empower pupils with SEND, placing them at the centre of decisions that impact their lives and recognising that they have expert knowledge because of their lived, embodied experiences. Anthony is also committed to supporting key stakeholders in schools such as teachers, special educational needs coordinators, learning support assistants, educational psychologists, and senior leaders to provide valuable and meaningful experiences of education for pupils with SEND.

Justin A. Haegele is Associate Professor, and Director of the Center of Movement, Health, & Disability, in the Department of Human Movement Sciences at Old Dominion University, USA. Broadly defined, his research focuses within the interdisciplinary field of adapted physical activity, with a primary interest in examining how disabled persons – in particular, blind, visually impaired and autistic individuals – experience physical activity participation, including school-based physical education. He is a Research Fellow with the Research Council of SHAPE and serves as Editor-in-Chief of *Adapted Physical Activity Quarterly* and *Quest*.

Routledge Focus on Sport Pedagogy
Series editor
Ash Casey, Loughborough University, UK

The field of sport pedagogy (physical education and coaching) is united by the desire to improve the experiences of young people and adult participants. The *Routledge Focus on Sport Pedagogy* series presents small books on big topics in an effort to eradicate the boundaries that currently exist between young people, adult learners, coaches, teachers and academics, in schools, clubs and universities. Theoretically grounded but with a strong emphasis on practice, the series aims to open up important and useful new perspectives on teaching, coaching and learning in sport and physical education.

Pedagogies of Social Justice in Physical Education and Youth Sport
Shrehan Lynch, Jennifer L. Walton-Fisette and Carla Luguetti

Learner-Oriented Teaching and Assessment in Youth Sport
Edited by Cláudio Farias and Isabel Mesquita

Physical Education Pedagogies for Health
Edited by Lorraine Cale and Jo Harris

Flipped Learning in Physical Education
Opportunities and Applications
Ove Østerlie, Chad Killian and Julia Sargent

Teaching Disabled Children in Physical Education
(Dis)connections between Research and Practice
Anthony J. Maher and Justin A. Haegele

For more information about this series, please visit: https://www.routledge.com/Routledge-Focus-on-Sport-Pedagogy/book-series/RFSPED

Teaching Disabled Children in Physical Education

(Dis)connections between Research and Practice

**Anthony J. Maher and
Justin A. Haegele**

LONDON AND NEW YORK

First published 2023
by Routledge
4 Park Square, Milton Park, Abingdon, Oxon OX14 4RN

and by Routledge
605 Third Avenue, New York, NY 10158

Routledge is an imprint of the Taylor & Francis Group, an informa business

British Library Cataloguing-in-Publication Data
A catalogue record for this book is available from the British Library

Library of Congress Cataloging-in-Publication Data
Names: Maher, Anthony J., author. | Haegele, Justin A., author.
Title: Teaching disabled children in physical education : (dis)
connections between research and practice / Anthony J. Maher and
Justin A. Haegele.
Description: Abingdon, Oxon ; New York, NY : Routledge, 2023. |
Series: Routledge focus on sport pedagogy | Includes bibliographical
references and index.
Identifiers: LCCN 2022029264 | ISBN 9781032008943 (hardback) |
ISBN 9781032008950 (paperback) | ISBN 9781003176282 (ebook)
Subjects: LCSH: Physical education for children with disabilities—
Study and teaching. | Physical education for children with
disabilities—Research.
Classification: LCC GV445 .M22 2023 | DDC 371.9/04486—dc23/
eng/20220625
LC record available at https://lccn.loc.gov/2022029264

ISBN: 978-1-032-00894-3 (hbk)
ISBN: 978-1-032-00895-0 (pbk)
ISBN: 978-1-003-17628-2 (ebk)

DOI: 10.4324/9781003176282

Typeset in Times New Roman
by codeMantra

Anthony:
For Katherine, Caleb, and Isla. Always.

Justin:
Everything I do is dedicated to Jane, Casey, and Emma.

Contents

Series Editor Introduction

Across this growing series of books, I'm increasingly being asked to sit up and listen. Some of the topics are more familiar, and the challenges are easier to adopt and meld into my existing work. In other cases, and this book is certainly one of those, I find myself reading with a sense of discomfort and a growing recognition of the need to change not only my practices but also the ways in which I think about disability and disabled students.

Throughout the book, Anthony J. Maher and Justin A. Haegele ask the reader to lay down their preconceptions and established notions of disability. They then challenge them (You and I) to consider afresh the ways in which disability has become socially constructed and addressed in our teaching of physical education. At the heart of this series is a focus on sport pedagogy, and this remit has been wholeheartedly taken up by Maher and Haegele and the result is a usable, articulate and meaningful exposition of disability. But they don't stop there. They offer up some ideas for changing practice to transform the experiences of disabled students in your care. This is a book to devour in one sitting and then use for months and years as you set out to include every student in PE so that they, and I quote, 'experience a sense of belonging, feeling accepted, and feeling valued.'

Ash Casey
16th June 2022

1 Foundational Information for Teaching Disabled Students in Physical Education

Introduction

This book centres on the role that research plays in the development and dissemination of pedagogical practices when teaching disabled students in physical education classes. Prior to engaging with chapters designed to examine, interrogate and problematise the empirical underpinnings of pedagogical practices in these areas, we first explore important foundational considerations that inform the how, and why, we teach disabled students in physical education contexts. Therefore, the aim of this chapter is to provide an overview of such foundational information that we believe is critical to understanding the ways in which disabled students are taught in physical education classes. We begin this chapter by discussing viewpoints towards disability to provide readers with general overviews of different conceptualisations of disability, and how these conceptualisations may influence the way in which teachers think about disabled students. We continue then to discuss educational settings and placements and conclude by discussing the concept of *inclusion* as an intersubjective experience, a contemporary conceptualisation we believe distinguishes it from simple conversations about educational placements. When engaging with this chapter, and subsequent chapters within this text, we caution readers not to consider these thorough, all-encompassing, or in-depth resources into each of the presented concepts. Rather, and more simply, we want to introduce readers to concepts that could, or perhaps should, influence ways of thinking about teaching disabled students in physical education classes, and how specific pedagogical practices may (or may not) be informed by research evidence.

DOI: 10.4324/9781003176282–1

What Is Disability?

Prior to engaging in conversations about the way in which disabled students have been educated in physical education classes, it is first important to consider what the term *disability* means. Disability is a complex, multi-dimensional phenomenon that has been understood in a variety of ways (Shakespeare, 2008). For example, early viewpoints on disability in Western Judea-Christian societies were framed in religious discourses, where impairments of the body were thought to be a product or act of a higher being (Fitzgerald, 2006; Haegele & Hodge, 2016; Haslett & Smith, 2020). These viewpoints have largely been discarded, as religious leaders have been replaced by doctors and scientists in contemporary culture as the *cognitive authority* in developing societal perceptions and values about disability (Humpage, 2007).

How disability is conceptualised today is important because it has implications for disabled people as well as service providers, such as physical educators (Haegele & Hodge, 2016). In this section of the chapter, we outline three different viewpoints towards disability that are among the most common internationally. In each section, we briefly summarise the disability model as well as implications ascribing to these models can have. Readers should note that the discussion that follows explores just some of many ways to consider disability. Hence, we urge our readers not to reduce understandings of disability into categories of convenience where one must place their beliefs solely within one of these buckets.

Medical Model

We begin with the medical model, which has been the most dominant way of understanding disability in Western cultures since replacing religious-informed viewpoints (Haslett & Smith, 2020). In the medical model, medical doctors are positioned as the cognitive authority, and disability is considered to be a medical problem that resides in the individual as a defect, or failure, of a body system that is abnormal and pathological (Haegele & Hodge, 2016). From this perspective, disability must be *fixed* to the greatest extent possible so persons can be *normal* and function within society (Brandon & Pritchard, 2011). *Fixed* is generally associated with psychological or medical interventions, often performed by nondisabled experts. In this viewpoint, limitations associated with *having* or *owning* a disability are viewed as a product of structural or functional deficiencies caused by physical, sensory, affective or cognitive *issues*, and these *issues* are inherently disabling, meaning no changes to the built environment or society can provide disabled people with equal opportunities as nondisabled others.

The medical model of disability permeates educational contexts within Western cultures. Of note, Haslett and Smith (2020) summarised that the medical model influences the language commonly used in physical education for disabled students (e.g., children with special needs), what types of interventions or educational programs are available and how educators and educational systems identify which individuals are in need of services. In addition, the medical model strongly influences the selection of students who are considered *disabled*, and how they qualify for services in many Western countries. In the United States and the United Kingdom, for example, there is a clear and notable reliance on diagnoses from medical professionals when attempting to gain access to services for disabled children in schools. This is a significant challenge for disabled children and their parents, in schools, as medical professionals act as gatekeepers whose opinions take priority over considerations for what the child or parent wants for their education. Additionally, the medical model can influence the way in which physical educators think about, and interact with, disabled students in their classes. That is, disability is a defining characteristic of those experiencing disability (Fitzgerald, 2006), and when disability is inherently bad (a view deeply embedded in this model), disabled students themselves can be viewed as faulty or undesirable. This perspective is reflected in how disabled students think about being treated in physical education classes, experiences that are typified by being discarded from activities, relegated to socially undesirable activities or socially isolated because of their disability (Haegele et al., 2021; Holland & Haegele, 2021).

UK Social Model

The UK social model of disability discourse is often presented as an opposing (although, this is a contentious statement) viewpoint of disability to the medical model. Unlike the medical viewpoint, the social model considers limitations associated with disability as being imposed on individuals with impairments by society (Haegele & Hodge, 2016; Palmer & Harley, 2012). Prior to continuing, it is critical here to explain some nuance with language. In the UK social model, the term *impairment* is used to describe an abnormality of the body or mind, such as a restriction or malfunction of a limb, whereas *disability* is used to describe the disadvantages that are caused by social institutions that do not take into account people who have impairments and exclude them from social life (Haslett & Smith, 2020). As such, there is nothing inherently disabling about having an impairment, but rather disability is imposed in addition to impairment by the way society restricts or excludes people from participating in their community. From this purview, disabled people should not be *fixed*, but rather disabled people should be valued and celebrated as part of society, and solutions to reduce disability should be focused on social change. The cognitive authority in this model are disabled academics and advocates.

Embedded in the social model is 'a deliberate attempt to shift attention away from the functional limitations of individuals with impairments onto the problems caused by disabling environments, barriers and cultures' (Barnes, 2020, p. 20). For those ascribing to the social model, impairment may be considered a constant in the disabled persons' lives, but disability need not be. This speaks to the influence that social model thinking may have in educational contexts, where physical educators could perhaps conceptualise and implement activities that respect and understand impairments experienced by their students without further disabling them by adding physical or social barriers to participation, or influencing and supporting hegemonic cultures that promote ablebodiedness as ideal and sporty (Haegele & Maher, 2021). It is important to note here, though, that the common perception that individually based medical, rehabilitative or educational interventions are not supported or valued by social model thinkers is untrue (Barnes, 2020). Rather, the model is concerned with ensuring that unneeded attention that is typically brought about with these interventions, which exacerbates focus on impairments, is diverted to empowering disabled people.

Social Relational Model

To date, the medical and social models of disability have gained most attention in physical education scholarship and practice. Despite this, dozens of other viewpoints towards disability exist and can inform the way in which physical educators interact with their students. Among those, the social relational model has been identified as a conceptually progressive consideration of disability. This viewpoint departs from prior understandings of disability because it adopts the perspective that disability is something that is imposed on top of, or in addition to, restrictions that are caused by one's impairment (Reindal, 2008). Thus, restrictions experienced by disabled persons, including restrictions in physical education classes, can be caused by both social reasons, such as discrimination, and by impairments of the body (Martin,

2013). As such, the social relational model stresses the effects of both one's impairment as well as social or structural limitations brought on by society (Reindal, 2008).

Tied to the social relational model of disability, and important for physical educators to consider, is the concept of psycho-emotional oppression. Psycho-emotional oppression is a form of social oppression that arises from negative social interactions between disabled and nondisabled persons and can be direct (i.e., explicit discrimination) or indirect (i.e., psycho-emotional consequences of exclusion from opportunities). The extant literature is riddled with examples of experiences of marginalisation, othering and bullying reflected by disabled students (Holland & Haegele, 2021) that encompass both direct and indirect psycho-emotional disablism. In our view, instances of psycho-emotional disablism are embedded into the fabric of contemporary physical education classes, and practitioners must be aware of the possibility of these potential negative consequences of their pedagogical practices. One clear strategy to understand how pedagogical practices might contribute to disablism, for physical educators and scholars alike, is to engage in meaningful conversations with disabled students and allow them to reflect upon their experiences in your classes.

Placement and Education for Disabled Students

The physical spaces or settings in which disabled students experience physical education are inextricably linked to the pedagogical practices that teachers select and implement for their education. These pedagogical decisions should, without a doubt, be informed by empirical research that has scrutinised the effectiveness or fidelity for education in these contexts. As such, the context in which activities are engaged in is of great importance when attempting to understand the (dis)connections between research evidence and practice. The physical space or setting that disabled students have received their education has changed dramatically in the past 100 years. As recent as the early 1900s, disabled children struggled to receive anything that resembled an education in many parts of the world. Some disabled students who experienced what were considered mild impairment may have been placed into general education contexts but were provided no support and therefore were unlikely to succeed (Karagiannis et al., 1996). Concurrently, those who were perceived to pose learning or behavioural challenges were simply discarded from classrooms and schools and denied an education (Wilson et al., 2020). The 1950s through the early 1970s saw the rise of special schools, which were designed to provide specialised and appropriate education for disabled students (e.g., schools for the blind children) that was unavailable in public schools at the time. Special schools, and self-contained classes within integrated schools, are still a central component of the education of many disabled students today (Maher & Fitzgerald, 2020; Pellerin et al., 2020; Pierce & Maher, 2020) and are favoured in some international contexts (Ahrbeck & Giese, 2020). Germany, for example, continues to maintain and value segregated schooling because it is believed that these schools provide more beneficial environments for disabled students (Ahrbeck & Giese, 2020). More so, though, calls have been made to discontinue or phase out special schools, in favour of integrating all disabled students into general education contexts, including in physical education (Wilson et al., 2020).

Today, more disabled students are integrated into the same educational context as their nondisabled peers than ever before. This shift towards integrated education aligns with articulations by the United Nationals Educational, Scientific, and Cultural Organization (2005), who state that disability of any kind cannot be a disqualifier from integrated education, as well as educational policies internationally (e.g., Individuals with Disabilities Act in the United States, the Special Educational Needs and Disability Act in the United Kingdom or the Brazilian Law on the Inclusion of Persons with Disabilities) that prioritise the integration of disabled students into general education classes (Heck & Block, 2019; Obrusnikova & Block, 2020). Movement towards integrated educational spaces has been influenced by the belief that educating all students in integrated, neighbourhood schools is 'a moral absolute that requires a single placement' (Kauffman et al., 2020, p. 5) and 'the right thing to do' (Yell, 1995, p. 389), whereas segregated schools designed to respond to the needs of students with particular educational needs in isolation from nondisabled peers should be dismantled or phased out (Kauffman et al., 2020; Slee, 2018). Highlighting this shift in educational placement, just over 90% of disabled students and those with special educational needs in England are educated in integrated schools (Department for Education, 2019). Moreover, recent data shows that the percentages of disabled students in the United States that spend at least 80% of their school day in integrated classes has doubled since 1990 (U.S. Department of Education, 2020).

While the shift towards integrated education has resulted in most disabled students being educated in heterogeneous settings with their nondisabled peers, these settings are not without concern. For example, scholars have cautioned that the shift towards integration has largely focused on the place of instruction rather than the quality of experiences within those places, as well as the ability of teachers to effectively instruct in those settings, which therefore can threaten the very meaning and purpose of education for disabled students (Kauffman et al., 2020; Shah, 2007). Others have pointed towards the potential for integrated contexts to be discriminatory, where disabled students may fail to gain full access to opportunities and curricula (Shah, 2007). In instances like this, it appears that although disabled students would be in the same physical space as their nondisabled peers, they would likely experience those spaces quite differently and perhaps at a disadvantage (Shah, 2007).

The shift towards integrated education is reflected in physical education, which has been identified as being among the first subjects within the school day where disabled students are permitted to join general education classes. Supporting this assertion, scholars internationally posit that most disabled students are currently enrolled in integrated physical education classes (Fitzgerald & Stride, 2012; Heck & Block, 2019). Importantly, tensions that have emerged regarding challenges associated with integrated education, in general (Kaufman et al., 2020), are also reflected in physical education scholarship (Fitzgerald & Stride, 2012; Haegele, 2019). For example, some scholarship suggests that integrated physical education classes can be discriminatory towards disabled students, particularly when physical educators are resistant to adapting activities and curricula to meet students' needs (Wilhelmsen et al., 2019), instead expecting disabled students to fit into existing classes (Haegele et al., 2021). In addition, it has been suggested that school administrators may manipulate placement decisions for financial or scheduling reasons, enrolling disabled students into integrated classes even when their educational needs may not be met within those contexts (Haegele, 2019).

Corresponding with the shift towards integration has been an increasing interest in the concept of inclusion. For some, it appears, inclusion has become a signpost for arguing for integrated education. However, to us, inclusion is largely a misunderstood and bastardised concept, that has resulted in physical educators making simple or superficial cosmetic adjustments to their pedagogical practices, many of which have little empirical support, to *check a box* and communicate the illusion of inclusion (Fitzgerald & Stride, 2012; Haegele & Maher, 2021). This behaviour is partially what inspired the purpose of this book, as making simple, observable adjustments to communicate the illusion of inclusion, which proliferate practice-based texts and resources, can unintentionally contribute to forms of exclusion and reinforce inequities in physical education classes. As such, it is important to us to help identify (dis)connections between practice and research support, particularly with regard to pedagogical practices that may be implemented with intentions of supporting inclusion, but may have adverse effects. Given the central role that the concept of inclusion plays in the physical education experiences of disabled students, and ambiguous or multiple meanings of the term, we unpack the concept of inclusion for readers in the final section of this chapter. Importantly, readers should note that there are multiple meanings to the term *inclusion* and therefore should seek to clarify the way in which authors utilise this term in other works before making claims of pedagogical practices supporting inclusive experiences.

Unpacking Inclusion

The term inclusion is inextricably linked to conversations about physical education and disabled students. Inclusion has been used in a variety of different ways in the physical education literature, oftentimes without clear or explicit definitions or meanings (Haegele, 2019). Clearly, based on the prior section of this chapter, we disagree with one common usage of this term, which is to describe a physical space or setting whereby disabled students are educated in the same context as their nondisabled peers. For us, the term integrated should be used rather than *inclusion* to describe physical locations that physical education classes are experienced (Haegele, 2019). The use of the term integration reflects values in the 1980s where the rights of disabled children to receive education in the same settings as their peers were emphasised (Obrusnikova & Block, 2020). However, to assume that education has improved within these settings, particularly in physical education classes, may be presumptuous (Haegele, 2019; Haegele & Maher, 2021).

For us, and as used throughout this text, inclusion should be conceptualised as an intersubjective experience which is characterised as feelings of belonging, acceptance and value (Haegele & Maher, 2021; Spencer-Cavaliere & Watkinson, 2010). With this conceptualisation, inclusion extends beyond an individual's physical presence within a given context, space or activity, and considers the individual's personal experiences within that space. With that, the feelings that disabled students have about their experiences are placed at the centre of this understanding of inclusion, rather than feelings or beliefs of the teacher. We believe this conceptualisation is well aligned with calls to amplify the voices of disabled students about their personal, lived experiences (Slee, 2018; Spencer-Cavaliere & Watkinson, 2010), as well as the *nothing about us, without us* movement that emphasises the role of disabled people in understanding their experiences.

There are several elements of this conceptualisation of inclusion that we find to be important for physical educators to consider. First, this understanding of inclusion allows for a broad application of the concept, where disabled students can experience these intersubjective experiences in a variety of settings. That is, with inclusion conceptualised as intersubjective experiences, persons are free to experience individual or shared feelings associated with inclusion in any host of contexts. In the setting of physical education, this may include integrated or self-contained settings, as well as other unique settings (such as those with small numbers of nondisabled students in classes with disabled students). We find this to be an important distinction, as research has identified that feelings associated with inclusion appear to be available in self-contained physical education contexts (Pellerin et al., 2020), perhaps to a greater degree than in integrated physical education settings (Holland & Haegele, 2021). This idea may be contentious in the United States (US) especially, however, given that many physical education scholars in that country equate integrated settings to inclusive experiences (Heck & Block, 2020; Lieberman et al., 2019) and may find experiencing inclusion outside of these settings to be idealistic or conceptually inconsistent. Second, considering inclusion as an intersubjective experience allows it to take on a fluid nature, which contrasts with traditional viewpoints towards inclusion that are often finite or fixed. With that, inclusion can take on a temporal dimension where students feel included at some times during a physical education class, and not included during others. We view this as an important feature for physical educators to consider, as ongoing input from students would be necessary to ensure experiences are inclusive, rather than *set it and forget it* pedagogical models that implement activities and assume inclusivity.

There are three central tenets of inclusion as an intersubjective experience: a sense of belonging, feeling accepted and feeling valued. Belonging, according to D'Eloia and Price (2018) and Mahar and colleagues (2013), is a fluid and contextual feeling of being connected to and cared for by others. Feeling needed, important, integral and respected within the group characterises most definitions of belonging. Feelings of belonging has been identified as a critical need within school-based contexts, including and perhaps especially for marginalised groups such as disabled students (Crouch et al., 2014). However, Crouch and colleagues (2014) suggest that ableism, alienation and teasing, which are all often experienced by disabled students in physical education (Holland & Haegele, 2021), are common threats to feelings of belonging. An important feature of belonging, as well as other tenets of inclusion, is that to eliminate threats to belonging, we must first understand belonging based on the views of disabled students themselves. As such, we argue that physical educators must actively engage with disabled students to understand if they experience feelings of belonging and must discard common assumptions that nondisabled adult stakeholders (e.g., physical educators) can understand and make judgements about these experiences without the students' input (Maher & Morley, 2020).

Feeling accepted is a peer-related concept that entails disabled students' perceptions of how others involve them in groups or communities (Shirazipour et al., 2017). The sense of community is central to feeling accepted, and one's existence within that community, and shared experiences within it, can influence acceptance, or lack thereof, within that community. It is important to note that seldom do people, disabled individuals or otherwise, experience universal acceptance within all groups and at all times. Rather, acceptance, or rejection, can change based on place, context and environment (Walker, 1999). Here, the spatial-temporal element of inclusion is clear, where in addition to feelings of inclusion fluctuating as time elapses, it can also change depending on the physical space and community within that space. According to Pesonen (2016), stakeholders whose professional values, beliefs and behaviours are aligned with creating welcoming and accepting contexts are crucial to the development and fostering of supportive climates. This reinforces the notion that gaining access to a physical space by itself is not enough for fostering feelings of acceptance, and that other social and pedagogical considerations must be made (Fitzgerald, 2005; Wilhelmsen et al., 2019). We argue that these points continue to reinforce the need to interrogating the (dis)connections between practices and research that supports those practices, particularly work that helps amplify the voices of disabled students within these contexts themselves.

Feeling valued, the final tenet of inclusion as an intersubjective experience, is generally the least explained in educational research. For us, feeling valued refers to the positive affective response arising from the confirmation that one's personal qualities and abilities are worthy and desirable. Importantly, there is a difference between knowing one's work and ability is valued, and feeling as though it is, and the latter rests largely with some form of praise or recognition from others (White & Mackenzie-Davey, 2003). Unsurprisingly, this is an important point for educators, who clearly play a crucial role in constructing feelings of value for disabled and nondisabled students within physical education contexts. That is, teachers are positioned as authoritative figures within educational contexts who can shape traditions and beliefs within those contexts (Maher & Fitzgerald, 2020). When teachers provide positive reinforcement and praise to disabled students within physical education settings, they are demonstrating that they are valuing the contribution that these students are making to the context, which can raise that student's sense of value, as well as nondisabled others' views about that student as well.

Conclusions

Within this chapter, we have provided an overview of foundational information intended to act as building blocks to help inform readers and prepare them to consume future chapters of this text. Here, we value introducing readers to important concepts that should influence the way in which they consider pedagogical practices within their educational context. Given what we have said in this chapter, we encourage teachers to critically reflect on their own beliefs about disability, focusing specifically on the ways and extent to which their beliefs and behaviours align with the models of disability and our consideration of the concept of inclusion. For us, this critical reflection is key for a better understanding of how, if at all, a teachers' curriculum decisions and pedagogical practices foster feelings of belonging, acceptance and value among disabled students in physical education. Of course, this needs to be accompanied by input from disabled students themselves because they have expert knowledge about how they feel during physical education. Admittedly, within this chapter, we are able only to provide superficial discussions of important topics. For readers who yearn for more in-depth and all-encompassing overviews of disability, educational placements and inclusion, concepts described in Chapter 1, we suggest engaging with *the Routledge Handbook of Disability Studies* (Watson & Vehmas, 2020), *Disability Studies: An Interdisciplinary Introduction* (Goodley, 2016), the *Routledge Handbook of Adapted Physical Education* (Haegele et al., 2020) and *Teaching Physical Education to Children with Special Educational Needs and Disabilities* (Vickerman & Maher, 2018).

References

Ahrbeck, B., & Giese, M. (2020). Inklusion – herausforderungen für die zweite phase der lehrkräftebildung. *Seminar, 26*(4), 5–17.

Barnes, C. (2020). Understanding the social model of disability: Past, present, and future. In N. Watson & S. Vehmas (Eds.), *Routledge handbook of disability studies* (2nd ed., pp. 14–31). Routledge.

Brandon, T., & Pritchard, G. (2011). "Bring fat": A conceptual analysis using three models of disability. *Disability & Society, 26*(1), 79–92. http://doi.org/10.1080/09687599.2011.529669

Crouch, R., Keys, C. B., & McMahon, S. D. (2014). Student-teacher relationships matter for school inclusion: School belonging, disability, and school transitions. *Journal of Prevention & Intervention in the Community, 42*(1), 20–30. https://doi.org/10.1080/10852352.2014.855054

D'Eloia, M. H., & Price, P. (2018). Sense of belonging: is inclusion the answer? *Sport in Society, 21*(1), 91–105. https://doi.org/10.1080/17430437.2016.1225819

Department for Education. (2019). *Special educational needs in England: January 2019.* London: DfE.

Fitzgerald, H. (2006). Disability and physical education. In D. Kirk, D. MacDonald, & M. O'Sullivan (Eds.), *The handbook of physical education* (pp. 752–766). London, UK: Sage Publications.

Fitzgerald, H., & Stride, A. (2012). Stories about physical education from young people with disabilities. *International Journal of Disability, Development and Education, 59*(3), 283–293. https://doi.org/10.1080/1034912X.2012.697743

Goodley, D. (2016). *Disability studies: An interdisciplinary introduction.* Sage.

Haegele, J. A. (2019). Inclusion illusion: Questioning the inclusiveness of integrated physical education. *Quest, 71*(4), 387–397. http://doi.org/10.1080/00336297.2019.1602547

Haegele, J. A., & Hodge, S. R. (2016). Disability discourse: Overview and critiques of the medical and social models. *Quest, 68*(2), 193–206. http://doi.org/10.1080/00336297.2016.1143849

Haegele, J. A., Hodge, S. R., & Shapiro, D. R. (Eds.). (2020). *The Routledge handbook of adapted physical education.* London, UK: Routledge.

Haegele, J. A., Kirk, T. N., Holland, S. K., & Zhu, X. (2021). 'The rest of the time I would just stand there and look stupid': Access in integrated physical education among adults with visual impairments. *Sport, Education & Society, 26*(8), 862–874. http://doi.org/10.1080/13573322.2020.1805425

Haegele, J. A., & Maher, A. J. (2021). Male autistic youth experiences of belonging in integrated physical education. *Autism, 26*(1), 51–61. http://doi.org/10.1177/13623613211018637

Haslett, D., & Smith, B. (2020). Viewpoints toward disability: Conceptualizing disability in adapted physical education. In J. A. Haegele, S. R. Hodge, & D. R. Shapiro (Eds.), *Routledge handbook in adapted physical education* (pp. 48–64). Routledge.

Heck, S., & Block, M. E. (2019). *Inclusive physical education around the world: Origins, cultures, & practices.* Routledge.

Holland, K., & Haegele, J. A. (2021). Perspectives of students with disabilities toward physical education: A review update 2014–2019. *Kinesiology Review, 10*(1), 78–87. https://doi.org/10.1123/kr.2020-0002

Humpage, L. (2007). Models of disability, work and welfare in Australia. *Social Policy & Administration, 41*(3), 215–231. https://doi.org/10.1111/j.1467-9515.2007.00549.x

Karagiannis, A., Stainabck, W., & Stainback, S. (1996). Rationale for inclusive schooling. In S. Stainback & W. Stainback (Eds.), *Inclusion: A guide for educators* (pp. 3–16). Paul H. Brookes Publishing Co.

Kauffman, J. M., Ahrbeck, B., Anastasiou, D., Badar, J., Felder, M., & Hallenbeck, B. A. (2020). Special education policy prospects: Lessons from social policies past. *Exceptionality*, 1–13. Epub ahead of print. https://doi.org/10.1080/09362835.2020.1727326

Lieberman, L. J., Brian, A., & Grenier, M. (2019). The Lieberman-Brian inclusion rating scale for physical education. *European Physical Education Review, 25*(2), 341–354. https://doi.org/10.1177%2F1356336X17733595

Mahar, A. L., Cobigo, V., & Stuart, H. (2013). Conceptualizing belonging. *Disability & Rehabilitation, 35*(12), 1026–1032. https://doi.org/10.3109/09638288.2012.717584

Maher, A. J., & Fitzgerald, H. (2020). The culture of special schools: Perceptions of the nature, purpose and value of physical education. *Educational Review*, 1–15. https://doi.org/10.1080/00131911.2020.1721437

Maher, A. J., & Morley, D. (2020). The Self stepping into the shoes of the Other: Understanding and developing empathy among prospective physical education teachers through a special school placement. *European Physical Education Review, 26*(4), 848–868. https://doi.org/10.1177%2F1356336X19890365

Martin, J. J. (2013). Benefits and barriers to physical activity for individuals with disabilities: a social-relational model of disability perspective. *Disability and Rehabilitation, 35*(24), 2030–2037. https://doi.org/10.3109/09638288.2013.802377

Obrusnikova, I., & Block, M. E. (2020). Historical context and definition of inclusion. In J. A. Haegele, S. R. Hodge, & D. R. Shapiro (Eds.), *Routledge handbook in adapted physical education* (pp. 65–80). Routledge.

Palmer, M., & Harley, D. (2012). Models and measurement in disability: An international review. *Health Policy and Planning, 27*(5), 357–364. https://doi.org/10.1093/heapol/czr047

Pellerin, S., Wilson, W. J., & Haegele, J. A. (2020). The experiences of students with disabilities in self-contained physical education. *Sport, Education, & Society*. E-publication ahead of print. https://doi.org/10.1080/13573322.2020.1817732

Pesonen, H. (2016). *Sense of belonging for students with intensive special education needs: An exploration of students' belonging and teachers' role in implementing support.* Helsinki: University of Helsinki.

Pierce, S., & Maher, A. J. (2020). Physical activity among children and young people with intellectual disabilities in special schools: Teacher and learning support assistant perceptions. *British Journal of Learning Disabilities, 48*(1), 37–44.

Reindal, S. M. (2008). A social relational model of disability: a theoretical framework for special needs education? *European Journal of Special Needs Education, 23*(2), 135–146. https://doi.org/10.1080/08856250801947812

Shah, S. (2007). Special or mainstream? The views of disabled students. *Research Papers in Education, 22*(4), 425–442. https://doi.org/10.1080/026715207016511288

Shakespeare, T. (2008). Debating disability. *Journal of Medical Ethics, 34*, 11–14. https://doi.org/10.1136/jme.2006.019992

Shirazipour, C. H., Evans, M. B., Caddick, N., Smith, B., Aiken, A. B., Martin Ginis, K. A., & Latimer-Cheung, A. E. (2017). Quality participation experiences in the physical activity domain: Perspectives of veterans with a physical disability. *Psychology of Sport & Exercise, 29*, 40–50.

Slee, R. (2018). *Inclusive education isn't dead, it just smells funny.* Routledge.

Spencer-Cavaliere, N., & Watkinson, E. J. (2010). Inclusion understood from the perspectives of children with disability. *Adapted Physical Activity Quarterly, 27*(4), 275–29. https://doi.org/10.1123/apaq.27.4.275

United Nationals Educational, Scientific, and Cultural Organization (UNESCO). (2005). *Guidelines for inclusion: Ensuring access to education for all.* Author.

U.S. Department of Education, Office of Special Education and Rehabilitative Services, Office of Special Education Programs. (2020). *42nd annual report to Congress on the implementation of the Individuals with Disabilities Education Act.* Author.

Vickerman, P., & Maher, A. J. (2018). *Teaching physical education to children with special educational needs* (2nd ed.). Routledge.

Walker, P. (1999). From community presence to sense of place: Community experiences of adults with developmental disabilities. *Journal of the Association of the Severely Handicapped, 24*(1), 23–32. https://doi.org/10.2511%2Frpsd.24.1.23

Watson, N., & Vehmas, S. (2020). *Routledge handbook of disability studies* (2nd ed.). Routledge.

White, M., & Mackenzie-Davey, K. (2003). Feeling valued at work? A qualitative study of corporate training consultants. *Career Development International, 8*(5), 228–234. https://doi.org/10.1108/13620430310497395

Wilhelmsen, T., Sorensen, M., & Seippel, O. N. (2019). Motivational pathways to social and pedagogical inclusion in physical education. *Adapted Physical Activity Quarterly, 36*(1), 19–41. https://doi.org/10.1123/apaq.2018-0019

Wilson, W. J., Haegele, J. A., & Kelly, L. E. (2020). Revisiting the narrative about least restrictive environment in physical education. *Quest, 72*(1), 19–32. https://doi.org/10.1080/00336297.2019.1602063

Yell, M. L. (1995). Least restrictive environment, inclusion, and students with disabilities: A legal analysis. *The Journal of Special Education, 28*(4), 389–404. https://doi.org/10.1177%2F002246699502800401

2 Research-Informed Practice in Physical Education

Introduction

Education research is now characterised by the breadth and diversity of its (cross)disciplinary commitments, theoretical positionings and methodological approaches. These shape decisions about what can and should be researched, how research should be done and what the results and findings mean and can be used for. For instance, one physical education scholar may be interested and see value in monitoring and evaluating the physical activity tendencies of autistic students in physical education to identify patterns of inequality, while another seeks to learn about how visually impaired students experience physical education by asking them questions to help improve the inclusiveness of teachers' pedagogical practices. While it is beyond the scope of this chapter to provide a full appraisal of research relating to disabled students in physical education, a superficial glance at the contents of the *Routledge Handbook of Adapted Physical Education* (Haegele, Hodge, and Shapiro, 2020) reveals the philosophical, theoretical, empirical and methodological diversity of this research field. In short, we argue that there is a reasonably strong research base for practitioners to draw on to support the decisions they make in schools when it comes to integrating disabled students in school life generally and physical education specifically. For instance, there is significant research relating to how disabled students experience and make sense of physical education in mainstream (e.g., Alves et al., 2020; Haegele & Maher, 2021) and special schools (e.g., Stride & Fitzgerald, 2011); how disabled people understand the inclusiveness of their experiences in integrated physical education classes (Haegele, Hodge, Zhu, et al., 2020; Haegele, Kirk, et al., 2021); how physical education teachers can foster a stronger and more productive relationship with special educational needs coordinators (e.g., Vickerman & Maher, 2018); senior

DOI: 10.4324/9781003176282-2

leader views on physical education in special schools (e.g., Maher & Fitzgerald, 2020); the role and responsibilities of learning support assistants (e.g., Maher, 2016); teacher beliefs about inclusion and what it involves in physical education (Haegele, Wilson, et al., 2021; Morley et al., 2021); beliefs about inclusive pedagogies in physical education (Maher et al., 2022; Overton et al., 2020; Wilson et al., 2020); the socialisation of physical education teachers into disability-related fields (Holland & Haegele, 2020) and the appropriateness of physical education initial teacher education for teaching students with special educational needs (Coates et al., 2020). The concern we have here relates to the difficulty connecting research and practice, or even researchers and practitioners. Before we explore the (dis)connections between research and practice, the next section clarifies what we mean by research-informed practice in physical education.

Defining and Justifying Research-Informed Practice in Physical Education

To clarify our position on and usage of *research-informed practice* we draw upon the work of Brown (2018) who considers it a combination of practitioner expertise and knowledge of the best external research and/or evaluation-based evidence. This definition is bound tightly to the Department for Education's standpoint on evidence-informed practice and policy, which suggests that schools and teachers in England can consider themselves research engaged if their practices, particularly their teaching, is *influenced by robust research* (Coldwell et al., 2017, p. 5). Therefore, an education practitioner can claim to be engaged in research-informed practice if, according to Burn and Mutton (2015), they gain insights from and draw upon educational research most closely aligned to their context-bound practice to make decisions within those contexts. For example, teacher practice becomes research informed when teachers use research generated knowledge about teaching disabled students in physical education to influence curriculum decisions, pedagogical actions and assessment strategies. Similarly, research findings can and should be drawn upon when senior leaders in schools decide how the disability-related budget should be spent because it can, for instance, give insight into the consequences of resource allocation for staff and students in different subject areas (see Maher & Macbeth, 2013). Moreover, research can be used when school leaders are considering the role and responsibilities of learning support assistants, who can play a crucial role in supporting or hindering the learning and development of disabled students (Goodwin et al., 2022).

These are just three of many examples illustrating the utility of research in schools. Many more will be offered throughout this book. Here, it is important to note, as Coldwell and colleagues (2017) did, that teaching is 'a complex, situated professional practice [that] draws on a range of evidence and professional judgment, rather than being based on a particular form of evidence' (p. 5).

While it is beyond the scope of this chapter to critically discuss hallmarks of quality in research, mainly because that can depend on the philosophical, theoretical and methodological alliances of those who engage with research, we consider Brown's (2018) *external research* and England's Department for Education's *robust research* (Coldwell et al., 2017) to relate to high-quality research that is original, rigorous and significant; that is qualitative and/or quantitative in nature and has been peer-reviewed before publication in an academic journal. While we return to this point throughout each chapter of the book, it is worth noting here that many of the practitioner-based texts found in practitioner journals fall outside the scope of our definition of high-quality research. Nonetheless, we do not expect teachers and other school practitioners to know how to judge high-quality research, have the time required to thoroughly unpick research methodologies and practices, or consider the credibility of the journals that publish such research. Rather, we hope that this book will go some way to developing your knowledge and understanding of the evidence base supporting research relating to teaching autistic students; Deaf students; students experiencing cognitive and learning difficulties; physically disabled students and visually impaired students so that you can make informed decisions about working with these groups of children and young people. Indeed, it is important to note that research cannot, and researchers should not, tell school practitioners what to do. Rather, research can and should be used by school staff to make informed decisions about, for instance, whole school strategy, pedagogy, curriculum and assessment.

A Rationale for Research-Informed Practice in Physical Education

The calls from government and universities for the teaching profession in England to be better informed about and actively engaged with research have increased over recent years (BERA/RSA, 2014; Coldwell et al., 2017; Flynn, 2019). These are based on claims, which are supported by research, that schools and teacher educators should use research as part of whole-school improvement plans that will impact positively on student outcomes. According to Burn and Mutton (2015), 'evidence from those contexts in which knowledge has been developed most systematically suggests that research-informed practice makes a very important contribution to school and system improvement' (p. 228). In this respect, it is crucial that physical education teachers can evaluate research findings so they can engage in well-informed, focused, pedagogical experimentation in which the learning and development of disabled students is carefully considered, monitored and reviewed. Our line of thinking here aligns with Brown (2018), who said:

> I firmly believe that educationalists engaging with evidence is socially beneficial. This is because policy decisions or teaching practice grounded in an understanding of what is or could be effective, or even simply an understanding of what is currently known, are likely to be more successful than those based on experience or intuition alone.
>
> (p. 1)

The penultimate section of this chapter provides some guidance on how to increase the ways and extent to which research influences practice. The next explores some of the key challenges to research informing practice in physical education.

Challenges to Research-Informed Practice in Physical Education

It is now well established in the academic literature that there are notable gaps between research and practice and, concomitantly, researchers and practitioners in schools. Dimmock (2016) refers to this as a hiatus between knowledge producers (academic researchers) and knowledge users (teachers). There a several reasons for this disconnect. One such reason is that the roles, values, expectations and professional constraints of researchers and stakeholders in schools do not always align well or complement each other. Thus, the endeavours of academics to translate and transfer research into practice must, according to Ellwood et al. (2013), be accompanied by an appreciation that stakeholders hold different sets of beliefs and expectations about education and research that require relationships to be negotiated. In short, there is a need for researchers to be sensitive to circumstances, experiences and expectations to increase the likelihood that research knowledge will be mobilised, schools will become (more) research engaged and practices research informed. For instance, many teachers rest their practices on experiences and pedagogical beliefs (Flynn, 2019), whether that be experiences of initial teacher education and/or as part of a community of practice within their former and/or current school. Thus, their teaching could be partly practice-informed-practice and partly ideology-informed-practice. Researchers and others involved in knowledge mobilisation therefore may have the difficult task of disrupting the often taken-for-granted beliefs and behaviours that have been developed by teachers and convincing them of the merits of using research to inform their practice. This becomes more difficult when research findings are incompatible with or even contrary to a teacher's ideological commitments and current teaching practices. In this regard, Cordingley (2008) argues that school stakeholders need to connect practically, emotionally and intellectually with context-specific research knowledge if they are to use it in their practice; research accounts need to resonate with them if it is to have any hope of influencing their beliefs about and actions towards teaching disabled students in physical education. Hence, those who write about research findings need to do so in a way that considers the personal and professional lives of teachers and views them as research consumers. At the same time, there is a need for researchers to place greater value on the tacit knowledge that teachers develop through their practice, especially when it has and/or is supported by experienced others as part of communities of practice within and across schools (Maher et al., 2022).

Brown (2014, 2018) is one of several scholars who has highlighted that for education practitioners, research has many of the characteristics of *consumer object* in that consuming research costs time, money and labour. For example, many research articles are behind expensive paywalls that require journal or article one-off payments or subscription fees. Open access journals and open access publication options have gone some way in shifting access costs away from research consumers, but this is not common practice in much research relating to education, physical education and/or disability. One solution to this is for teachers to contact researchers directly to request post-acceptance, pre-typeset journal articles, but this requires teachers to know how to source relevant research articles, which may not always be the case. Schools that commission and/or conduct their own research also incur a time, financial and labour cost, as does the professional development required for staff to learn how to source and use research to inform their practice (Brown, 2014, 2018). Hence, there is an obvious need to connect researchers and teachers to ensure that some of their challenges to developing a culture of research-informed practice in schools are minimised. The next section will consider ways in which the link between research and practice can be strengthened.

Connecting Research and Practice in Physical Education Teacher Education

Given the many challenges to connecting research and practice, it is crucial that both practitioners and researchers consider carefully how they can work together to ensure that research knowledge is mobilised to and in schools, and that practitioners are able to consume that knowledge and make sense of how it connects with their everyday activities. Initial teacher education is crucial in creating the expectation among pre-service teachers that their practice should be both practice- and research-informed. Similarly, initial teacher education can be used to develop the knowledge, skills, experience and confidence required to interpret and use research in a way suitable to the contextual needs of teachers, something we know teachers struggle to do (Coldwell et al., 2017). While being far from exhausted as an area of research in and of itself, the relationship between research and practice in initial teacher education has been explored internationally (e.g., Flores, 2017; Marcondes et al., 2017; Valeeva & Gafurov, 2017; Van Nuland, 2011). In some countries, such as Finland, research is woven through most aspects of teacher education programmes, from it being an explicit part of the curriculum through bespoke research methods modules, to its application influencing practical activities and the field experiences of pre-service teachers (see Hökkä & Eteläpelto, 2014). When discussing what they term the *research-based model* of teacher education in Finland, Hökkä and Eteläpelto (2014) highlighted the study of research methods and the writing of a master's dissertation aiming at training 'autonomous and reflective teachers capable of adopting a research-oriented attitude towards their work' (p. 42). France (Lapostolle & Chevaillier, 2011) and the Netherlands (Snoek et al., 2017) are two other European countries who seem to have embraced research-informed practice in teacher education. In other countries, according to Flores (2018), research is either non-existing or on the periphery. In England, the picture is mixed. The ITT Core Content Framework, which sets out a training package for pre-service teachers as a minimum entitlement, does not focus on research-informed practice, instead suggesting that teacher training providers 'should ensure their curricula encompass the full entitlement described in the ITT Core Content Framework, as well as integrating additional analysis and critique of theory, research and expert practice as they deem appropriate' (DfE, 2019, p. 4). Thus, teacher educators have the autonomy to weave research-informed practice through curricula, or not. Hence, the extent and way in which research is a part of initial teacher education in England can largely depend on the expertise and prioritised of the institution educating the pre-service teachers, and the nature and purpose of the relationship they have with schools.

Despite calls in this book and elsewhere for a greater focus on embedding research into the professional socialisation of teachers, it is worth noting that much of the earlier research relating to preparing pre-service teachers to teach disabled students and those with special educational needs highlight a perceived failing of government and teacher educators to preparing them as inclusive practitioners (see Vickerman & Maher, 2018). This mostly related to claims that there was a complete lack of focus on teaching disabled students in physical education, and when disability, diversity and inclusion were covered it was typically through a tokenistic lecture-based *theoretical* session about *the models of disability, concepts of inclusion* and/or *how to modify and adapt activities* that was given to trainee teachers of all subjects, leaving many pre-service physical education teachers unable to understand how to apply the knowledge to practice (Morley et al., 2005). Interestingly, pre-service physical education teachers also called for much more hands-on experience working with disabled students – for practice-informed practice – because the first time many were exposed to disabled students, particularly those with more significant impairments, was when they were newly qualified teachers (Coates, 2012; Holland & Haegele, 2020). While research suggests that pre-service physical education teachers are now getting much more experience working with disabled students (Morley et al., 2021) than they were in the past (Morley et al., 2005), with some gaining experience in a special school (Coates et al., 2020; Maher et al., 2022), no research has explored the ways and extent to which theoretical knowledge and research relating to disabled students in physical education shapes physical education initial teacher education.

From what we do know from the research discussed above is that research becomes infused through teacher education, and increases the likelihood that teachers will know how to and be able to use research knowledge and conduct their own research when: there is a research methods module embedded within the curriculum, which also allows them to plan and conduct a research project that is tied to teaching practice; research and theory are applied to practical activities; pre-service teachers are given the time and support to critically reflect on and discuss the relationship between theory and practice during practical activities; research and theory shape the field or placement experiences of pre-service teachers and is supported by professional mentors and tutors.

Teacher Continued Professional Development

While much of the research relating to research-informed practice in education focuses on initial teacher education, it is of course crucial that governments, schools and teachers themselves invest in teacher continued professional development to ensure that knowledge and skills have currency. Teacher professional learning and development, therefore, is fertile ground for research knowledge mobilisation to help teachers to learn how to use research about disability and inclusion to inform their pedagogical actions. According to Davidson and Jensen (2009), those professional development programmes that adopt a research-informed, enquiry-oriented approach are considered most useful and thus rated most highly by teachers (Davidson & Jensen, 2009). It is also worth noting that teachers' learning about and use of research findings, together with opportunities to conduct their own collaborative research inquiries as part of their professional development, has been found to impact positively on student outcomes (Burn & Mutton, 2015; Cordingley, 2008; Leask & Younie, 2013). It is thus crucial that continued professional development programmes do more than expose teachers to research knowledge; they also need to help them to develop the skills to apply that knowledge and support teachers to become researchers themselves. Here, it is noteworthy that hardly any of the continued professional development experienced by physical education teachers in research by Morley et al. (2021) focused on supporting disabled students, mostly because of its low status when it came to school priorities. Therefore, there is a need for universities and its staff with research expertise in this area to do more to reach out and foster stronger, collaborative and reciprocal relationships with teachers in schools to provide professional development opportunities that are mutually beneficial. Indeed, whilst such a collaborative approach will help teachers to explore whether, if at all, their practice has an empirical basis, it will also enable researchers to learn more about how their research can and should be applied (Flynn, 2019). While the focus is primarily on teacher professional development, the same can be said about university researchers working with senior leaders and learning support assistants in schools, given that both groups say that they struggle to provide appropriate support to physical education teachers and disabled students in physical education (Maher, 2016, 2018) and thus may benefit from developing their knowledge and understanding of the evidence base of different support strategies. In this respect, most of the school senior leaders and learning support staff in research conducted by Maher and Macbeth (2013) called for professional development opportunities relating to supporting disabled students in physical education because of their recognition of its importance and their own limitations.

Teacher-led research, characterised as research planned and conducted by teachers either alone or in collaboration with researchers or other staff in a school, has been proposed as action research and self-study (Craig, 2009). According to Santos et al. (2020) teaching and research are bound together and should be considered a natural part of a teacher's role given that self-questioning is integral to teaching and research. Being a teacher requires diverse skills, and self-investigating of practice is one of them. If we accept the claim made by Kincheloe (2003) that researching school and teacher practices allows teachers to know and understand the complexity of their role and working environment, leading to more informed and appropriate decisions, then all teachers should commit to being researchers. While ITE and CPD processes are crucial to ensuring that teachers develop the knowledge and competencies to be researchers, it is important that the schools in which they work are research engaged to ensure that support mechanisms are in place. This aligns with the work of Dimmock (2016), who argues for the need to develop research engaged schools, which become places for research design, methodology and application to help schools tackle practical problems. Research suggests that schools that commit to being research engaged and have a strategic plan to that effect can shift school practices from superficial guidance about school improvement to a learning culture where staff work collaboratively and share a commitment to understanding what works, how, when and why (Godfrey, 2016; Greany, 2015). Another key benefit of fostering a school culture that values teachers as researchers is that it has been found to increase the number of applications for teaching posts, work satisfaction and staff retention (Godfrey, 2016). For this ideal to become a reality, buy-in from senior leaders in crucial. Indeed, according to a Department for Education report conducted by Coldwell et al. (2017),

> in the most highly research-engaged schools, senior leaders played a key role, acting as intermediaries and facilitators of access to, engagement with and use of research evidence for staff in their schools. To do so, they often had direct access to research producers….

It is therefore apparent that researchers must try to connect with and engage senior leaders in schools, as well as teachers, to increase the impact that research has on school practices.

Conclusion

This chapter sought to clarify our usage of the terms research and practice, before considering the connection between both in physical education. As part of this, we emphasised the importance of schools being research engaged, research knowledge being mobilised in schools, and researchers and practitioners working together to develop the research-base relating to teaching disabled students and supporting teachers to ensure that their practice is research-informed. Indeed, there is an obvious need for researchers and school practitioners to work together to ensure that schools are research engaged and that physical education teachers can source, conduct and use research to improve the educational experiences of disabled students.

References

Alves, M. L., Grenier, M., Haegele, J. A., & Duarte, E. (2020). "I didn't do anything, I just watched": Perspectives of Brazilian students with physical disabilities toward physical education. *International Journal of Inclusive Education, 24*(10), 1129–1142. https://doi.org/10.1080/13603116.2018.1511760

BERA/RSA. (2014). *Research and the teaching profession: Building the capacity for a self-improving education system, final report of the BERA-RSA inquiry into the role of research in teacher education.* BERA/RSA.

Burn, K., & Mutton, T. (2015). A review of 'research-informed clinical practice' in initial teacher education. *Oxford Review of Education, 41*(2), 217–233. https://doi.org/10.1080/03054985.2015.1020104

Brown, C. (2014). *Evidence informed policy and practice: A sociological grounding.* Bloomsbury.

Brown, C. (2018). *Achieving evidence-informed policy and practice in education: Evidenced.* Emerald Publishing.

Craig, C. J. (2009). Teacher research and teacher as researcher. In L. J. Saha & A. G. Dworkin (Eds.), *International handbook of research on teachers and teaching* (Vol. 21, pp. 61–70). Springer.

Coates, J. (2012). Teaching inclusively: Are secondary physical education teachers sufficiently prepared to teach in inclusive environments? *Physical Education and Sport Pedagogy, 17*(4), 349–365. https://doi.org/10.1080/17408989.2011.582487

Coates, J. K., Harris, J., & Waring, M. (2020). The effectiveness of a special school experience for improving preservice teachers' efficacy to teach children with special educational needs and disabilities. *British Educational Research Journal, 46*, 909–928. https://doi.org/10.1002/berj.3605

Coldwell, M., Greany, T., Higgins, St., Brown, C., Bronwen, M., Stiell, B., Stoll, L., Willis., B., & Burns, H. (2017). *Evidence-informed teaching: an evaluation of progress in England: Research report*. DfE.

Cordingley, P. (2008). Research and evidence-informed practice: Focussing on practice and practitioners. *Cambridge Journal of Education, 38*(1), 37–52. https://doi.org/10.1080/03057640801889964

Davidson, M., & Jensen, B. (2009). Creating effective teaching and learning environments: First results from TALIS. OECD. Retrieved from http://www.oecd.org/education/school/43023606.pdf

Department for Education (DfE). (2019). *Initial teacher training (ITT): core content framework*. London: DfE. Retrieved from https://www.gov.uk/government/publications/initial-teacher-training-itt-core-content-framework

Dimmock, C. (2016). Conceptualising the research-practice-professional development nexus: Mobilising schools as 'research engaged' professional development learning communities. *Professional Development in Education, 42*(1), 36–53. https://doi.org/10.1080/19415257.2014.963884

Ellwood, P., Thorpe, R., & Coleman, C. (2013). A model for knowledge mobilisation and implications for the education of social researchers. *Contemporary Social Science Journal, 8*(3), 191–206. https://doi.org/10.1080/21582041.2012.751496

Flores, M. A. (2017). Editorial. Practice, theory and research in initial teacher education. *European Journal of Teacher Education, 40*(3), 287–290. https://doi.org/10.1080/02619768.2017.1331518

Flores, M. A. (2018). Linking teaching and research in initial teacher education: Knowledge mobilisation and research-informed practice. *Journal of Education for Teaching, 44*(5), 621–636. https://doi.org/10.1080/02607476.2018.1516351

Flynn, N. (2019). Facilitating evidence-informed practice. *Teacher Development, 23*(1), 64–82. https://doi.org/10.1080/13664530.2018.1505649

Godfrey, D. (2016). Leadership of schools as research-led organizations in the English educational environment: Cultivating a research engaged school culture. *Educational Management Administration & Leadership, 44*(2), 301–321. https://doi.org/10.1177%2F1741143213508294

Goodwin, D., Rossow-Kimball, B., & Connolly, M. (2022). Students' experiences of paraeducator support in inclusive physical education: Helping or hindering? *Sport, Education and Society, 27*(2), 182–195. https://doi.org/10.1080/13573322.2021.1931835

Greany, T. (2015). How can evidence inform teaching and decision making across 21,000 autonomous schools? Learning from the journey in England. In C. Brown (Ed.), *Leading the use of research & evidence in schools* (pp. 11–29). IOE Press.

Haegele, J. A., Hodge, S. R., & Shapiro, D. (Eds.). (2020). *Routledge handbook of adapted physical education*. Routledge.

Haegele, J. A., Hodge, S. R., Zhu, X., Holland, S. K., & Wilson, W. J. (2020). Understanding the inclusiveness of integrated physical education from the perspectives of adults with visual impairments. *Adapted Physical Activity Quarterly, 37*(2), 141–159. https://doi.org/10.1123/apaq.2019-0094

Haegele, J. A., Kirk, T. N., Holland, S. K., & Zhu, X. (2021). 'The rest of the time I would just stand there and look stupid': Access in integrated physical education among adults with visual impairments. *Sport, Education & Society, 26*(8), 862–874. https://doi.org/10.1123/apaq.2019-0094

Haegele, J. A., & Maher, A. J. (2021). Male autistic youth experiences of belonging in integrated physical education. *Autism, 26*(1), 51–61. https://doi.org/10.1123/apaq.2019-0094

Haegele, J. A., Wilson, W. J., Zhu, X., Bueche, J. J., Brady, E., & Li, C. (2021). Barriers and facilitators to inclusion in integrated physical education: Adapted physical educators' perspectives. *European Physical Education Review, 27*(2), 297–311. https://doi.org/10.1123/apaq.2019-0094

Holland, S. K., & Haegele, J. A. (2020). Socialization experiences of first year adapted physical education teachers with a master's degree. *Adapted Physical Activity Quarterly, 37*(3), 304–323. https://doi.org/10.1123/apaq.2019-0094

Hökkä, P., & Eteläpelto, A. (2014). Seeking new perspectives on the development of teacher education: A study of the Finnish context. *Journal of Teacher Education, 65*(1), 39–52. https://doi.org/10.1177%2F0022487113504220

Kincheloe, J. L. (2003). *Teachers as researchers: Qualitative inquiry as a path to empowerment* (2nd ed.). Routledge Falmer.

Lapostolle, G., & Chevaillier, T. (2011). Teacher training in France in the early 2000s. *Journal of Education for Teaching, 37*(4), 451–459. https://doi.org/10.1080/02607476.2011.611014

Leask, M., & Younie, S. (2013). National models for continuing professional development: The challenges of twenty-first-century knowledge management. *Professional Development in Education, 39*(2), 273–287. https://doi.org/10.1080/19415257.2012.749801

Maher, A. J. (2016). Special educational needs in mainstream secondary school physical education: Learning support assistants have their say. *Sport, Education and Society, 21*(2), 262–278. https://doi.org/10.1080/13573322.2014.905464

Maher, A. J. (2018). "Disable them all": SENCO and LSA conceptualisations of inclusion in physical education. *Sport, Education and Society, 23*(2), 149–161. https://doi.org/10.1080/13573322.2016.1162149

Maher, A. J., & Fitzgerald, H. (2020). The culture of special schools: The nature, purpose and value of physical education. *Educational Review* [online first]. https://doi.org/10.1080/00131911.2020.1721437

Maher, A. J., & Macbeth, J. L. (2013). Physical education, resources and training: The perspective of special educational needs coordinators working in secondary schools in North-West England. *European Physical Education Review, 20*(1), 90–103. https://doi.org/10.1177%2F1356336X13496003

Maher, A. J., Thomson, A., Parkinson, S., Hunt, S., & Burrows, A. (2022). Learning about inclusive pedagogies through a special school placement. *Physical Education and Sport Pedagogy, 27*(3), 261–275. https://doi.org/ 10.1080/17408989.2021.1873933

Marcondes, M. I., Leite, V., & Ramos, R. (2017). Theory, practice and research in initial teacher education in Brazil: Challenges and alternatives. *European Journal of Teacher Education, 40*(4), 326–341. https://doi. org/10.1080/02619768.2017.1320389

Morley, D., Banks, T., Haslingden, C., Kirk, B., Parkinson, S., van Rossum, T., Morley, I. D., & Maher, A. J. (2021). Physical education teachers' views of including pupils with special educational needs and/or disabilities: A revisit study. *European Physical Education Review, 27*(2), 401–418. https://doi. org/10.1177%2F1356336X20953872

Morley, D., Bailey, R., Tan, J., & Cooke, B. (2005). Inclusive physical education: Teachers' views of including pupils with special educational needs and/or disabilities in physical education. *European Physical Education Review, 11*(1), 84–107. https://doi.org/10.1177%2F1356336X05049826

Overton, H., Wrench, A., & Garrett, R. (2017). Pedagogies for inclusion of junior primary students with disabilities in PE. *Physical Education and Sport Pedagogy, 22*(4), 414–426. https://doi.org/10.1080/17408989.2016.1176134

Santos, A., Polidoro João, T., Porto Filgueiras, I., & dos Santos Freire, E. (2020). Research on the teaching practice itself in physical education classes: Implications and challenges perceived by a teacher-researcher. *Sport, Education and Society, 26*(7), 759–772. https://doi.org/10.1080/13573322.2020.1802712

Snoek, M., Bekebrede, J., Hanna, F., Creton, T., & Edzes, H. (2017). The contribution of graduation research to school development: Graduation research as a boundary practice. *European Journal of Teacher Education, 40*(3), 361–378. https://doi.org/10.1080/02619768.2017.1315400

Stride, A., & Fitzgerald, H. (2011). Girls with learning disabilities and 'football on the brain'. *Soccer & Society, 12*(3), 457–470. https://doi. org/10.1080/14660970.2011.568111

Valeeva, R., & Gafurov, I. (2017). Initial teacher education in Russia: Connecting theory, practice and research. *European Journal of Teacher Education, 40*(3), 324–360. https://doi.org/10.1080/02619768.2017.1326480

Van Nuland, S. (2011). Teacher education in Canada. *Journal of Education for Teaching, 37*(4), 409–421. https://doi.org/10.1080/02607476.2011.611222

Vickerman, P., & Maher, A. J. (2018). *Teaching physical education to children with special educational needs and disabilities* (2nd ed.). Routledge.

Wilson, W. J., Theriot, E. A., & Haegele, J. A. (2020). Attempting inclusive practice: Perspectives of physical educators and adapted physical educators. *Curriculum Studies in Health & Physical Education, 11*(3), 187–203. https://doi.org/10.1080/25742981.2020.1806721

3 Teaching Autistic Students in Physical Education

Background and Context

Since the early 2000s, no impairment has gained more attention internationally than autism. This attention is at least partially informed by the high, and increasing, prevalence of autism diagnoses. While it is challenging to gather an up-to-date international prevalence of autism diagnoses, country-based estimates are common. In the United Kingdom, for example, there has been a 787% exponential increase in the incidence of autism diagnoses between 1998 and 2018 according to Russell and colleagues (2021). This equates to approximately 65,000 autism diagnoses in 2018, most of which (about 61%) are among school-aged youth. Similar trends are occurring elsewhere. For example, in the United States, the prevalence rate of autism diagnoses has increased 241% since 2000, and today approximately 1 in 44 American children are diagnosed with autism (Maenner et al., 2021). Within these rates, boys are four times as likely to be diagnosed with autism than girls, and over 95% of autistic children have co-occurring impairments or health conditions, commonly including epilepsy, gastrointestinal issues or sleep disturbances. For our purposes, it is noteworthy that autistic children and young people are often identified as physically inactive (Healy et al., 2017), having high rates of overweight and obesity (Healy et al., 2019) and as displaying aberrant kinetic and kinematic movements during walking and running (Bennett et al., 2021). Of particular importance, autistic students have reported having challenging or meaningless experiences within physical education contexts, which are typified by bullying, overstimulation or social isolation, particularly in integrated settings with their non-autistic peers (Haegele & Maher, 2021, 2022; Lamb et al., 2016).

DOI: 10.4324/9781003176282-3

Overview of Disability

Within schools, autism is generally thought of through a bio-medical deficit lens where autistic students are *treated* to reduce and eliminate *undesirable* characteristics or behaviours. This is discussed later in this chapter, regarding several pedagogical strategies (e.g., applied behaviour analysis, discrete trial training) that are commonly recommended and implemented based on this ideology. First identified by Dr Leo Kanner in 1943, autistic people were previously diagnosed with mental illness and, more specifically, schizophrenia before formal criteria for autism were introduced. Today, the International Classification of Diseases 11 (ICD-11) defines autism as a neurodevelopmental disorder characterised by persistent deficits in the ability to initiate and sustain reciprocal social interaction and social communication, and a range of restricted, repetitive and inflexible patterns of behaviour, interests or activities that are clearly atypical or excessive for an individual's age or social context (ICD, 2022). According to the ICD-11, the onset of the disorder occurs during the developmental period, but characteristics may not fully manifest until later. Importantly, while there are numerous theories about what causes autism, no definitive answers have been reached. However, the National Institutes of Health (2018) characterise autism as a neurodevelopmental disorder that is attributed to both genetics and the environment. What is known, though, is that despite early falsified and subsequently retracted publications by Wakefield and colleagues (1998), as well as ever-common media and celebrity sensationalism, there is no link between vaccinations and autism.

An important discourse about autism from autistic advocates and scholars has begun to challenge the negative framing of autism as a pathologised abnormality and related efforts to remediate behaviour to fit an idealised norm (Milton, 2012). This movement, which has adopted the political slogan *Nothing about us, without us*, has suggested that these archaic ideologies cause damage and harm to autistic persons themselves (Milton, 2012) and assert that it is time to challenge these understandings of autism to diminish existing stereotypes and assumptions. This movement has highlighted 'the need for researchers to listen to the voices of people with autism themselves (or to proxy reports for those who cannot self-advocate) and to pay far greater attention to the qualitative experience of adults with autism' (Howlin, 2021, p. 4300). By amplifying autistic voices, scholars and practitioners can gain a greater understanding of possible ways to minimise barriers to engagement in many aspects of life, including in school-based contexts like physical education. This movement has previously influenced our work (see Haegele & Maher, 2021, 2022) and has guided scholars and educators in further valuing the words and experiences of autistic people when developing and implementing pedagogical practices. As such, when exploring empirical work to (or not to) support pedagogical suggestions, particular focus is placed on research that amplifies the voices of autistic students within physical education contexts throughout this chapter.

Aim and Purpose

As noted, autistic students have gained considerable attention over the past 20 years, which has also come with an influx of academic scholarship pertaining to pedagogical strategies within education settings, including physical education. In this chapter, we review and critique pedagogical strategies promoted in practice-based articles and textbooks to teach autistic students. In doing so, we centre our conversation around non-fiction narratives about Mrs Smither, a physical educator, and an autistic student in her classes, Caleb. Mrs Smither has found herself at the centre of our story, purposely, as we are cognizant that seldom is the agency of autistic students emphasised in their physical education experiences. As such, here we show a glimpse of how Mrs Smither navigates physical education decisions for her new student, Caleb. Caleb has been featured in our work elsewhere (Haegele & Maher, 2021) and reappears here in a unique setting and new school. Following each short narrative, we discuss and critique each pedagogical strategy that is depicted within the story utilising existing practical and empirical literature.

Routines and Structure

Mrs Smither, entering her first year teaching physical education at Middleton High School, has just learned, days before school begins, that she'll have Caleb, an autistic boy, in her class. Knowing that Caleb will be joining her class, Mrs Smither is keen to think about and consider ways to ensure that he has a meaningful experience within her class. To gain some ideas, she's enlisted the help of physical educators from other schools, as well as some instructors from her time at university, and asked questions about what they might do. Curiously, she's heard the term structure often now, many times from peers who have had more experience teaching autistic students. She has also been told several times that establishing a clear routine will be helpful for Caleb. With those marching orders, Mrs Smither jumps into action, exploring different ways to ensure the environment is predictable for Caleb, while still integrating him into the classes' activities with his peers. Before her classes even begin, and prior to Caleb entering the room, she has colour coded various stops in the room, constructed new barriers with bright signs and marked a spot for him to sit when the class is receiving instruction. She only hopes that it 'works.'

As autism has become more prevalent internationally, so have recommendations for teaching autistic students within schools, including in physical education. Among the most commonly used terms that have emerged when considering pedagogical practices for autistic children in physical education are routine and structure (Felzer-Kim et al., 2021; Gordon & Pennington, 2022; Weiner & Grenier, 2020). According to Hodge and colleagues (2012), routines and structure can be thought of as providing information with set beginning and end points that allow predictability and help reduce sensory overload. It has been suggested that, by establishing routines and providing information in a structured manner, students can learn new skills and behaviours more efficiently, respond appropriately with the maximum extent of independence possible and perform with minimal need for verbal directions from instructors (Felzer-Kim et al., 2021; Houston-Wilson, 2020; Roth, 2013). Because of the perception of routine and structure having utility in teaching autistic children within integrated physical education settings, suggestions to embed routines and structure within classroom settings, as well as examples of how to do so, are, seemingly, everywhere. Some common suggestions include utilising visual schedules to help communicate the day's events so autistic students can understand what's expected of them that day, as well as the use of timers to communicate the end of activities (Fittipaldi-Wert & Mowling, 2009; Grenier, 2014). Other examples suggest that teachers develop a home base as a starting point so students know where they must be to begin instruction and to create concrete physical boundaries using cones or labels so autistic students know where they are permitted to move within a space (Hodge et al., 2012). Ironically, one suggestion by Hodge and colleagues, to keep the home base within close proximity to the instructor, is criticised in another practice-oriented text by Alexander and Schwager (2012) as something that doesn't work 'because children with ASD [autism spectrum disorders] don't perceive the nonverbal messages those strategies are intended to communicate' (p. 204).

Despite the propensity of scholars and practitioners to discuss structure and routine as critical and central concepts when teaching autistic children and young people in physical education (Felzer-Kim et al., 2021; Gordon & Pennington, 2022; Hodge et al., 2012), the evidence to support it within this context is relatively unfounded. Even in instances where recommendations conflict, there is seemingly little research support for either side. It is feasible that perhaps these recommendations are extensions from other fields, such as special education, however assuming transferability to physical education contexts, given the unique particularities of this context, is short-sighted. Interestingly, when scanning through the reference lists of many of the practice-based resources that suggest routines and structure as sound pedagogical strategies, it is evident, and problematic, that most resources that are informing these ideas are simply previously published practice-based papers or texts. Said another way, most of the suggestions that are made in these practice-based papers are informed by other authors making similar recommendations, apparently ignoring the necessity for empirical evidence to support these suggestions. Indeed, there is a distinct absence of the high-quality contextually dependent research that is advocated by Brown (2018) and Coldwell et al. (2017) to support research-informed recommendations about how best to structure learning environments and use routines to support the learning and development of autistic students in physical education. This is problematic for numerous reasons, perhaps foremost that we, as scholars, are communicating to teachers how to teach autistic students based on what is equivalent to academic rumours, without any attempt to support these rumours by collecting, analysing and disseminating data. This is not to say that these strategies may not be effective in supporting autistic students within physical education contexts. However, without data to support it we (scholars) may be speaking out of line when it comes to our understanding of what pedagogical practices to adopt when teaching autistic youth. Perhaps this (dis)connection is even more pressing and concerning given that autistic young people have described challenges engaging with the often-chaotic nature of physical education classes (Haegele & Maher, 2021, 2022; Lamb et al., 2016). With that, strategies that could effectively reduce chaos, such as establishing structure and routine, may be welcomed additions through the eyes of autistic people. But, without some work to gather evidence of their feasibility and effectiveness, it appears that this particular pedagogical suggestion is evidence of (dis)connections between research and practice.

Applied Behaviour Analysis (ABA)

In addition to speaking with other physical educators, Mrs Smither has reached out to a few friendly special educators whom she knows to ask for advice when teaching autistic students. To her surprise, each of the teachers refers her to the concept of ABA, a phrase unfamiliar to Mrs Smither that is seemingly well-known by special educators. Each person she speaks to says the same thing, 'if you can implement ABA, you can help reduce some behaviours'. *Without knowing Caleb well yet, or understanding what the special educators mean by* 'reducing behaviours', *Mrs Smither does a bit of digging to learn more. Luckily, there are sections in each text she owns that discusses autism in physical education, and each of those discusses ABA. Perhaps, she wonders, could this be helpful for Caleb?*

To think of ABA as one teaching approach may be reductive, given many pedagogical practices have roots in this understanding of behaviour. For example, some teaching practices that are influenced by ABA include functional behaviour assessments, peer interventions, discrete trail training, teaching for generalisation and prompting (Felzer-Kim et al., 2021; Holland et al., 2019). Here, though, we will speak in general terms when discussing ABA, as this is common within practice-based texts and articles suggesting its applicability for teaching autistic students in physical education (Grenier, 2014). Rooted in behaviourism (Skinner, 1953), ABA can be defined as 'the systematic application of behavioural principles to change socially significant behaviour to a meaningful degree' (Alberto & Troutman, 2013, p. 403). Practically speaking, ABA operates with the understanding that the environment has an important impact on the presentation of behaviours through the use of stimuli (i.e., items that influence behaviour to happen) and reinforcements (i.e., increases or maintains a response to a stimulus). According to Houston-Wilson (2020), the 'premise behind this model is that when an appropriate behaviour is followed by positive reinforcement, the appropriate behaviour will be repeated' (p. 200). While there is a rich history of ABA and its application to physical education environments (Ward & Barrett, 2002), suggestions for its application to teaching autistic students in physical education are fairly recent. When discussed in practice-based texts, ABA is commonly discussed as an effective means for learning new skills (Houston-Wilson, 2020) and understanding and altering *problematic* behaviours (Felzer-Kim et al., 2021).

Despite the rich history of ABA within research in physical education contexts among non-autistic people (Lee & Ward, 2020; Ward & Barrett, 2002), as well as many studies exploring ABA principles and their utilisation in exercise contexts for autistic individuals (Felzer-Kim & Hauck, 2020; Ketcheson et al., 2021), little has been done focusing on autistic students within physical education context, specifically. One such study that we are aware of that was rooted in principles of ABA was from Ward and Ayvazo (2006) and demonstrated the utility of class-wide peer tutoring in physical education for autistic youth.

With that, many would point towards the expansive research in other educational, recreational and exercise settings in which research using ABA has been more thoroughly employed to support its utilisation in physical education contexts for autistic students. However, given our focus on physical education settings and empirical support within this context, we would encourage practitioners to exercise caution when generalising these practices without deep consideration. Of further importance, ABA has recently been problematised for ethical issues, where scholars have suggested that while ABA is sometimes thought of as a *best practice* or the *best treatment* for autistic people, it may also represent systematic violations of bioethics and may *cause more harm than good* (Bellon-Harn et al., 2022; Kupferstein, 2018; Wilkenfeld & McCarthy, 2020). For example, Wilkenfeld and McCarthy (2020) note that ABA may be unethical because it violates the autonomy of students who are subjected to it for a variety of reasons, including the attempt to eliminate certain preferences or desires that the student may have, undermining their autonomy to choose. Others have criticised practices rooted in ABA, largely focusing on discrete trail training, as being emotionally abusive for autistic individuals (Bellon-Harn et al., 2022) and as being an antecedent for post-traumatic stress disorder (Kupferstein, 2018). For us, and with our focus on understanding the perspectives of autistic people specifically, we have growing concern about ABA within physical education contexts given these alarming assertions.

Video Modelling

Caleb's now been in Mrs Smither's class for a month or so and has had varied experiences. Some lessons he is quite engaged, while others he finds himself sitting on the side-line. This week, Caleb's class is dancing. Caleb loves to dance, and he's excited to learn a new dance called 'the Cha Cha Slide'. It's a line dance, and he's heard it before at his cousin's wedding, among other places. When the dance starts, Caleb's excitement to dance overshadows his attention to the words and dance moves, and he finds himself falling behind. Dejected, he sits down on the bench, and waits for the song to end. Mrs Smither appears to notice the issue and asks Caleb to join her further away from the radio in a far corner of the gymnasium. She presents Caleb an iPad, with the same video that rest of his class is using to learn the dance. She tells him that he can use this instead and explains that he can stop and start instruction as he likes. As Mrs Smither walks back to the rest of the class, Caleb begins to explore the iPad, and the video player, to see how this new device might help him to learn a dance he's excited to do.

Video modelling, a pedagogical strategy that has emerged in physical education contexts as technology continues to be integrated in this space, is the occurrence of a behaviour by an observer that replicates a behaviour that is demonstrated by a model on a video (Colombo-Dougovito, 2015). Typically, video modelling includes a model (e.g., peer, sibling) who is video-recorded while engaging in a desired behaviour, and an individual who watches the video demonstration and attempts to mimic the behaviour (Case & Yun, 2015). Various examples of video modelling have been described in the physical education literature, including basic video modelling (i.e., showing a video of someone besides the learner performing a task), video self-modelling (i.e., using the learner as the model) and video prompting (i.e., breaking skills down into steps and creating pauses to prompt specific skills) (Colombo-Dougovito, 2015; Grenier, 2014; Judge & Morgan, 2020). Practice-based resources suggest video modelling as an effective, and cost efficient, tool for helping autistic students understand complex skills (Grenier, 2014). Of further benefit, videos are portable, so learning can occur outside of the physical education space when videos are played at home or after school. Video modelling has also been recommended as a practice that can be implemented without the direct supervision of a physical education teacher, and perhaps with a teacher aid, given that instructions are inherent to the video being watched (Haegele & Kozub, 2010). This can allow autistic students to view the video when away from larger groups, which may also help to direct attention to the correctly performed elements of the skill on the video without potential distracting elements (Obrusnikova & Rattigan, 2016).

Recommendations to use video modelling as a pedagogical practice are supported by a significant literature base which demonstrates that video instructions, sometimes presented on an iPad, are favoured among autistic students and can be helpful in assisting them in acquiring scripted verbal skills (Flores et al., 2012; Shukla-Mehta et al., 2010). However, and despite the number of practice-based articles that advocate for the use of video modelling in physical education contexts, data within these settings to support this pedagogical strategy are limited (Case & Yun, 2018). This was highlighted by Case and Yun (2018), who noted that given this popularity, 'it is important that empirical evidence exists that supports the use of video modeling and any positive associated effects such as improved skill performance and acquisition, administration time, and convenience among professionals' (p. 2). With that, a few recent studies have examined the utility of video modelling in physical education settings for autistic students. Interestingly, most studies in this area have found video modelling, as well as video presentation apps, to have little to no effect on the motor performance of autistic youth in physical education settings (Bittner et al., 2017, 2018; Case & Yun, 2018). This is clearly problematic, as practice-based articles and texts continue to support and advocate for the use of video modelling in physical education contexts for autistic students despite null findings. This finding is well aligned with assertions by Case and Yun (2018), who suggested that 'there are currently no studies that empirically support the use of video modeling strategies to improve motor skills among children with ASD' (p. 8). As such, we suggest practitioners exercise caution when implementing, and scholars do the same when suggesting, the use of video modelling in physical education contexts, particularly when the rationale is based entirely on improving the motor skills of autistic students.

Conclusion

This chapter has provided a brief overview of understandings of autism before exploring, using vignettes and discussions of the extant literature, pedagogical strategies often presented for teaching autistic students in integrated physical education. Here, we provide narratives about using structure and routines, ABA and video modelling when engaging autistic students in physical education classes. Problematically, while each of these pedagogical strategies are often depicted as sound advice for physical educators when teaching autistic students, empirical support within that context is lacking. Perhaps alarmingly, available research on some of these strategies (i.e., video modelling) has shown no positive effects, where emerging evidence on others (i.e., ABA) is demonstrating deleterious effects for autistic people. This raises significant questions about recommendations that are evident in the practice-based literature, and what contributes to these recommendations. For us, it is critical that we engage directly with autistic people, in the frame of *nothing about us, without us*, to gain an understanding of their wants, needs and desires, within integrated physical education contexts.

References

Alberto, P. A., & Troutman, A. C. (2013). *Applied behavior analysis for teachers* (9th ed.). Pearson.

Alexander, M. G. F., & Schwager, S. M. (2012). *Meeting the physical education needs of children with autism spectrum disorder.* NASPE.

Bellon-Harn, M. L., Boyd, R. L., & Manchaiah, V. (2022). Applied behavior analysis as treatment for autism spectrum disorders: Topic modeling and linguistic analysis of Reddit posts. *Frontiers in Rehabilitation Sciences, 2,* Article 682533. https://doi.org/10.3389/fresc.2021.682533 Bennett, H. J., Ringleb, S. I., Bobzien, J., & Haegele, J. A. (2021). Walking lower extremity biomechanics of adolescents with autism spectrum disorder. *Journal of Biomechanics, 119,* 110332. https://doi.org/10.1016/j.jbiomech.2021.110332

Bittner, M., Myers, M., Silliman-French, L., & Nichols, D. (2018). Effectiveness of instructional strategies on the motor performance of children with autism spectrum disorder. *Palaestra, 32*(2), 36–42.

Bittner, M., Rigby, B. R., Silliman-French, L., Nichols, D. L., & Dillon, S. R. (2017). Use of technology to facilitate physical activity in children with autism spectrum disorder: A pilot study. *Physiology & Behavior, 177,* 242–246. https://doi.org/10.1016/j.physbeh.2017.05.012

Brown, C. (2018). *Achieving evidence-informed policy and practice in education: Evidenced.* Emerald Publishing.

Case, L., & Yun, J. (2015). Visual practices for children with autism spectrum disorders in physical activity. *Palaestra, 29*(3), 21–25.

Case, L., & Yun, J. (2018). Video modeling and test of gross motor development-3 performance among children with autism spectrum disorder. *European Journal of Adapted Physical Activity, 11,* 1–10. https://doi.org/10.5507/euj.2018.009

Coldwell, M., Greany, T., Higgins, St., Brown, C., Bronwen, M., Stiell, B., Stoll, L., Willis., B., & Burns, H. (2017). *Evidence-informed teaching: an evaluation of progress in England: Research report.* DfE.

Colombo-Dougovito, A. (2015). Successful evidence-based practices for autism spectrum disorder and their use for the development of motor skills in physical education. *Palaestra, 29*(2), 34–41.

Felzer-Kim, I. T., Campbell, H., Vallabheneni, N., Peterson, A., & Hauck, J. L. (2021). Working with children with autism in general physical education: Useful applied behavior analysis concepts. *Journal of Physical Education, Recreation, & Dance, 92*(9), 50–55. https://doi.org/10.1080/07303084.2021.1977741

Felzer-Kim, I. T., & Hauck, J. L. (2020). How much instructional time is necessary? Mid-intervention results of fundamental movement skills training within ABA early intervention centers. *Frontiers in Integrative Neuroscience, 14,* Article 24. https://doi.org/10.3389/fnint.2020.00024

Flores, M., Musgrove, K., Renner, S., Hinton, V., Strozier, S., Franklin, S., & Hill, D. (2012). A comparison of communication using the Apple iPad and a picture-based system. *Augmentative and Alternative Communication, 28*(2), 74–84. https://doi.org/10.3109/07434618.2011.644579

Fittipaldi-Wert, J., & Mowling, C. M. (2009). Using visual supports for students with autism in physical education. *Journal of Physical Education, Recreation, & Dance, 80*(2), 39–43. https://doi.org/10.1080/07303084.2009.10598281

Gordon, V., & Pennington, C. G. (2022). Tips for including individuals with autism in physical education. *Journal of Physical Education, Recreation, & Dance, 93*(1), 58–60. https://doi.org/10.1080/07303084.2022.2006021

Grenier, M. (2014). *Physical education for students with autism spectrum disorder: A comprehensive approach.* Human Kinetics.

Haegele, J. A., & Kozub, F. M. (2010). A continuum of paraeducator support for utilization in adapted physical education. *Teaching Exceptional Children Plus, 6*(5), Article 2.

Haegele, J. A., & Maher, A. J. (2021). A creative non-fiction account of autistic youth integrated physical education experiences. *Disability & Society.* Epub ahead of print. https://doi.org/10.1080/09687599.2021.2007361

Haegele, J. A., & Maher, A. J. (2022). Male autistic youth experiences of belonging in integrated physical education. *Autism, 26*(1), 51–61. https://doi.org/10.1177%2F13623613211018637

Healy, S., Aigner, C., & Haegele, J. A. (2019). Prevalence of overweight and obesity among US youth with autism spectrum disorder. *Autism, 23*(4), 1046e1050. https://doi.org/10.1177%2F1362361318791817

Healy, S., Haegele, J. A., Grenier, M., & Garcia, J. M. (2017). Physical activity, screen-time behavior, and obesity among 13-year olds in Ireland with and without autism spectrum disorder. *Journal of Autism & Developmental Disorders, 47*, 49–57. https://doi.org/10.1007/s10803-016-2920-4

Hodge, S. R., Lieberman, L. J., & Murata, N. M. (2012). *Essentials of teaching adapted physical education: Diversity, culture, and inclusion.* Scottsdale, AZ: Holcomb Hathaway.

Holland, S. K., Holland, K., Haegele, J. A., & Alber-Morgan, S. (2019). Making it stick: Teaching students with autism to generalize physical education skills. *Journal of Physical Education, Recreation & Dance, 90*(6), 32–39. https://doi.org/10.1080/07303084.2019.1614120

Houston-Wilson, C. (2020). *Autism spectrum disorder.* In J. P. Winnick & D. L. Porretta (Eds.), *Adapted physical education and sport* (7th ed., pp. 195–212). Champaign, IL: Human Kinetics.

Howlin, P. (2021). Adults with autism: Changes in understanding since DSM-111. *Journal of Autism and Developmental Disorders, 51*, 4291–4308. https://doi.org/10.1007/s10803-020-04847-z

Judge, J., & Morgan, K. M. (2020). Video modeling: Strategies to support physical activity in children with autism spectrum disorder. *Palaestra, 34*(2), 37–42.

Ketcheson, L., Felzer-Kim, I. T., & Hauck, J. L. (2021). Promoting adapted physical activity regardless of language ability in young children with autism spectrum disorder. *Research Quarterly for Exercise & Sport, 92*(4), 813–823. https://doi.org/10.1177/0031512517743823

Kupferstein, H. (2018). Evidence of increased PTSD symptoms in autistics exposed to applied behavior analysis. *Advances in Autism, 4*(1), 19–29. https://doi.org/10.1108/AIA-08-2017-0016

Lamb, P., Firbank, D., & Aldous, D. (2016). Capturing the world of physical education through the eyes of children with autism spectrum disorder. *Sport, Education & Society, 21*(5), 698–722. https://doi.org/10.1080/13573322.2014.941794

Lee, J., & Ward, P. (2020). Single-subject research designs in APE. In J. A. Haegele, S. R. Hodge, & D. R. Shapiro (Eds.), *Routledge handbook of adapted physical education* (pp. 197–212). Routledge.

Maenner, M. J., Shaw, K. A., Bakian, A. V., Bilder, D. A., Durkin, M. S., Esler, A., et al. (2021). Prevalence and characteristics of autism spectrum disorder among children aged 8 years – autism and developmental disorders monitoring network, 11 sites, United States, 2018. *MMWR Surveillance Summaries, 70*(SS-11), 1–16. http://dx.doi.org/10.15585/mmwr.ss7011a1

Milton, D. (2012). On the ontological status of autism: The 'double empathy problem'. *Disability & Society, 27*(6), 883–887. https://doi.org/10.1080/09687599.2012.710008

National Institutes of Health (NIH). (2018). *Autism fact sheet.* Author.

Obrusnikova, I., & Rattigan, P. J. (2016). Using video-based modeling to promote acquisition of fundamental motor skills. *Journal of Physical Education, Recreation, & Dance, 87*(4), 24–29. https://doi.org/10.1080/07303084.2016.1141728

Roth, K. (2013). Adapt with apps. *Journal of Physical Education, Recreation & Dance, 82*(4), 4–6.

Russell, G., Stapley, S., Newlove-Delgado, T., Salmon, A., White, R., Warren, F., Peason, A., & Ford, T. (2021). Time trends in autism diagnosis over 20 years: A UK population-based cohort study. *The Journal of Child Psychology and Psychiatry*, Epub head of print: https://doi.org/10.1111/jcpp.13505

Shukla-Mehta, S., Miller, T., & Callahan, K. J. (2010). Evaluating the effectiveness of video instruction on social and communication skills training for children with autism spectrum disorders: A review of the literature. *Focus on Autism and Other Developmental Disabilities, 25*(1), 23–36. https://doi.org/10.1177%2F1088357609352901

Skinner, B. F. (1953). *Science and human behavior.* Macmillan.

Wakefield, A. J., Murch, S. H., Anthony, A., Linnell, J., Casson, D. M., Malik, M., Berelowitz, M., Dhillon, A. P., Thomson, M. A., Harvey, P., & Valentine, A. (1998). RETRACTED: Ileal-lymphoid-nodular hyperplasia, non-specific colitis, and pervasive developmental disorder in children. *The Lancet, 351*(9103), 637–641.

Ward, P., & Ayvaso, S. (2006). Classwide peer tutoring in physical education: Assessing its effects with kindergartners with autism. *Adapted Physical Activity Quarterly, 23*, 233–244. https://doi.org/10.1123/apaq.23.3.233

Ward, P., & Barrett, T. (2002). A review of behavior analysis research in physical education. *Journal of Teaching in Physical Education, 21*(3), 242–266. https://doi.org/10.1123/jtpe.21.3.242

Weiner, B., & Grenier, M. (2020). Sensory balancing strategies for students with autism spectrum disorder. *Journal of Physical Education, Recreation & Dance, 91*(8), 21–28. https://doi.org/10.1080/07303084.2020.1798308

Wilkenfeld, D. A., & McCarthy, A. M. (2020). Ethical concerns with applied behavior analysis for autism spectrum "disorder". *Kennedy Institute of Ethics Journal, 30*(1), 31–69. https://doi.org/10.1353/ken.2020.0000

4 Teaching Deaf Students in Physical Education

Background and Context

Hearing loss is the second most prevalent impairment in the United Kingdom (UK) (Kim et al., 2018). According to research conducted by Action on Hearing Loss in 2015, about one in six, or approximately 11 million people, were found to experience some form of hearing loss in the UK. The prevalence of hearing loss increases with age. Approximately 6.4 million of the 11 million who experienced hearing loss were aged 65 and above, and about 3.7 million were of working age (16–64 years). By 2035, it is estimated that 15.6 million people will have some form of hearing loss in the UK due to an aging population (Action on Hearing Loss, 2015). Research by the Consortium for Research in Deaf Education (CRIDE, 2019) suggests that there are at least 53,954 Deaf children across the UK, 78% of whom attend mainstream school. Roughly 22% of Deaf children were identified as having an additional learning need in 2019 (CRIDE, 2019). Research highlights that Deaf young people typically leave school with fewer qualifications and are less likely to go on to further study, gain employment and be promoted in work when compared to hearing people (Luft, 2015). For our purposes, it is noteworthy that Deaf children and young people are, when compared to hearing age-peers, much more likely to have poorer balance (De Kegel et al., 2011; Majlesi et al., 2014), experience delays in motor development (Rine et al., 2000) and be less physically active (Li et al., 2018; Lobenius-Palmér et al., 2018).

Overview of Disability

In general, there are bio-medical and socio-cultural definitions of deafness. Historically, and even today, deafness is considered a bio-medical deficit of the individual, attributed to hearing loss and impairment. From

DOI: 10.4324/9781003176282-4

this perspective, emphasis is placed on treating, even curing, hearing impairment. This aligns with the medical model of disability, whereby the individual and their impairment is cast as the problem that needs to be fixed and normalised, typically through medical intervention (Barnes et al., 1999). The goal here is to assimilate people with hearing impairments into speaking and hearing worlds through, for instance, the use of cochlear implantation and a focus on speech therapy and oralism so that Deaf young people can lip read and speak (Friedner & Block, 2017). However, a social understanding of deafness focuses on the ways and extent to which the social attitudes and behaviours that shape organisational policies and practices, serve to disadvantage and oppress Deaf people. From this perspective, teachers should be interested in how school and physical education policies, strategies, curriculum decisions, pedagogical actions and assessment arrangement, albeit unintentionally, favour hearing young people at the expense of Deaf young people.

Many members of the Deaf community, however, have rejected both medical and social model understandings of deafness and instead reconceptualised it as a cultural-linguistic facet of identity that cannot be explained as either entirely medical or social in nature (Hodge et al., 2012). Deafness, from this purview, refers to a socio-linguistic minority group, with a shared identity and culture tied to collective beliefs and values about, and experiences relating to, deafness. Here, you may have noticed that we use a capital *D* when referring to Deaf people and the Deaf community as it aligns with the work of critical Deaf studies scholars (e.g., Padden & Humphries, 1988). Specifically, the capitalisation marks a challenge and ultimate rejection of deafness as impairment and an affirmation of Deaf culture and Deaf identity (Friedner & Helmreich, 2012).

Aim and Purpose

The aim of this chapter is to critique the strategies discussed and promoted in academic literature and used to teach and support Deaf pupils in physical education. To do this, creative non-fiction accounts, which centre on Sarah, a Deaf pupil, and Ms Patel, her physical educator, are provided relating to the experiences of Sarah in a mainstream, integrated physical education class. The strategies used in these accounts, which represent notable best practices that are commonly presented in best practice papers and taught in pre-service teacher education programmes, are then discussed in relation to the academic literature supporting them before the evidence-base is critiqued. We hope that this approach supports teachers and other practitioners to make evidence-informed decisions when working with Deaf students. This aligns with our goal of encouraging schools to be more research engaged and supporting teachers as researchers.

Consider Your Positioning

Ms Patel walked slowly and purposely to the group. She spotted Sarah sat on the periphery. She casually changed her direction of travel, making sure not to look directly at Sarah before stopping in her general area so that they were facing each other. Girls, face me please, *she said. The class quickly spun around to face Ms Patel.* Good. Thank you, *she added.* Today, we are practicing dribbling the football. *Then, Ms Patel set out five cones, before skilfully dribbling the ball through the cones towards the group, who were sat patiently watching her.* Keep the ball close to your feet so you don't lose control and use the inside then outside of your foot, *she explained.* Now, it's your turn, *she added, after finishing the drill.*

Positioning can be important when teaching Deaf students who may rely heavily on lip reading verbal instructions and observing skills and techniques being demonstrated. According to practitioner-oriented papers by Lieberman (2016) and Schultz et al. (2013), Deaf students who lip read need to be able to see the faces of teachers when they speak to understand what they are being asked to do. This can become tricky when teachers are demonstrating a skill or technique so positioning again is important to consider. According to Fiorini and Manzini (2018), teachers where possible should perform demonstrations, like Ms Patel did, while facing and moving towards Deaf students if the demonstration is accompanied by verbal instruction. If no verbal instruction is involved, Reich and Lavay (2009) advocate for demonstrating the technique while facing away from the Deaf student so that they can mirror or model the demonstrator's actions. In this respect, Reich and Lavay (2009) suggest that teachers could ask other students to model the technique while the teacher provides verbal instruction and feedback. While this is an established practice in physical education, we caution teachers to carefully consider the support needs and abilities of the Deaf students because those who lip read would be unable to read verbal instructions and observe demonstrations simultaneously.

Teaching in a sports hall, gymnasium or outdoors on a field is not the same as in a classroom. Physical education learning environments are much more dynamic, interactive and frenetic (Maher, 2010). Therefore, physical education teachers often find themselves constantly on the move, trying to position themselves so they can observe what it is happening during activities, and so that they can be seen and heard by all students, especially when relaying instructions and giving feedback (Maher, 2020). This is especially important when working with Deaf students because these students, unlike most of their hearing peers, rely much more on their eyes to interpret non-verbal cues. Deaf students need to be able to see faces to lip read and bodies to see demonstrations. Therefore, it is crucial that teachers talk to Deaf students about the best ways to position themselves throughout activities. In this respect, trial and error is key. Physical education teachers need to experiment with their positioning, reflect on it, and discuss it with deaf students afterwards. Teacher and pupil reflections are an important form of evidence that can be used when evaluating teaching practices. Researchers can use systematic observations to analyse teacher positioning. Moreover, technology may add a different dimension, using video analysis and thermal mapping to systematically track and/or use to support teachers and pupils to reflect on movement patterns. Regardless of the focus of the research, there is an obvious need for high-quality research that explores teacher positioning in physical education when teaching Deaf students because the evidence-base supporting this practice is notably weak.

Use Non-verbal Cues

Ms Patel had arranged for teams of four students to play each other for five minutes per game in a mini basketball tournament. It was three points a win, one point for a draw and zero for a loss. She had selected the teams herself to ensure that they were even in relation to ability, but also placed Sarah with a player that she had a positive relationship with. Before the tournament commenced, Ms Patel explained to all the players that she would use colourful bibs to communicate with them during the games. Blue means foul, yellow means that there are 30 seconds remaining and red means stop, the game has finished*, she said.* Right, Beth, your team [which included Sarah] is up first, and you're playing Natalia's team*, she added.*

According to Maher (2020), Deaf students often rely on visual pedagogies; that is, teaching and learning approaches that utilise the learners' eyes. Therefore, practitioner-based papers have emphasised that visual cues can be important when working with Deaf students. While demonstrations are useful forms of visual pedagogy, they are not the only. According to non-empirical papers by Roth et al. (2016) and Fiorini and Manzini (2018), teachers should create signals that are easy to recognise and see when communicated at a distance in busy physical education environments. This was the intention of Ms Patel's brightly coloured bids. In this respect, Maher (2020) also encourages physical education teachers to carefully consider how other students as teammates may use non-verbal cues to gain the attention of a Deaf teammate and relay information about how and where they want to receive the ball and changes in tactics. In addition, Reich and Lavay (2009) suggest that physical education teachers should print new vocabulary and instructions. For instance, when introducing an unfamiliar concept or exercise, write it on a whiteboard or print a copy as a reference point. Unfamiliar equipment can also be labelled so teachers can point to the words as they progress through an activity (Reich and Lavay, 2009). These approaches are in keeping with Barboza et al.'s (2015) work relating to the theory of dynamic systems, which they relate to a Deaf person's interaction with the visual environment in which they are inserted.

Like other areas, there is a distinct dearth of scholarly and practitioner research about the types of non-verbal cues that are best for relaying instruction, giving feedback or motivating to Deaf students during physical education lessons. Deaf children relay on sight, as well as other senses, for developing meaning (Bauman, 2008). However, we should not assume that all types of non-verbal cues, such as smiling or frowning, pointing with fingers or hands or waving brightly coloured flags or bibs are appropriate in all contexts and situations with all Deaf students. Instead, there is a need to systematically explore what works best, with whom and in what situations and circumstances. Similar can be said about physical education teachers' use of demonstrations. While demonstrations are an established and important pedagogical tool in physical education, they are often accompanied by verbal instruction and learned and performed for hearing students, which is not always appropriate for some Deaf students (Maher, 2020). Therefore, there is a need for researchers and teachers to understand and develop best practice guidelines for using demonstrations with Deaf students that are based on high-quality research. Research that uses systematic observations, teacher reflections and pupil voice will be key for developing understanding and guidelines.

Working with Interpreters

The school has money available to employ Trish, an interpreter. Ms Patel knows some basic signs but not enough to communicate complex information to Sarah. Ms Patel had suggested that she, Sarah, and Trish meet before the first physical education lesson of the new school year to discuss how the three of them can work together. Ms Patel is nervous; she has never worked with a Deaf student who requires an interpreter. So, how can we make this work, *asks Ms Patel?* Well, there are a few important things, *replies Trish verbally, while signing her words to Sarah.* First, when you are talking to the class, and Sarah especially, make sure you look at them and not me. You only need to look at me when you are talking to me. It is also useful if you use the names of the person or people you are talking to so that I can relay that to Sarah, *Trish added. At that point, Sarah begins to sign to Trish.* Good point, Sarah, *says Trish.* Sarah asked that you not talk too quickly and leave a short break in between instructions so that I have time to sign and she to interpret, *Trish added.*

The purpose of an interpreter for Deaf students is to facilitate successful communication between teacher and pupil (Schultz et al., 2013). To increase the likelihood of that happening, Lieberman (2016) suggests that teacher, interpreter and Deaf student should meet prior to teaching commencing to discuss and agree upon roles and communication strategies and etiquette. In that respect, it is important that the Deaf student is actively involved in these discussions because they will know their own communication preferences best. Of course, like all modes of communication, it may take some time and effort to develop strategies that work best for all involved. Again, the positioning of the interpreter is said to be key to successful communication. According to Lieberman (2016), this should be either next to the teacher or in the most appropriate spot to convey instructional information to the Deaf student when necessary. Others have advocated for teachers to learn and use sign-language in their lessons. Mourão (2008) claims that teachers who use sign language fluently maintain clear dialogues with Deaf students, which impacts positively on the confidence of those students.

It is crucial to note that there is no empirical research about how best teachers, students and interpreters can navigate their interactions and relationships, or the most effective ways of supporting each other to perform their roles. Similarly, there is an urgent need to systematically explore the impact of interpreters on the social, emotional, physical and cognitive learning and development of Deaf students in physical education, given that this ties to the purpose and value of subject (Bailey, 2018; Maher & Fitzgerald, 2020). While most of the limited literature relating to the use of interpreters focuses on communication between Deaf student and teacher, there is a need to explore how if at all interpreters help or hinder the development of prosocial relationships between Deaf students and hearing peers. In this respect, it is noteworthy that research suggests that the presence of learning support assistants can act as a barrier to disabled students and those with special educational needs developing positive relationships with their age peers (Goodwin et al., 2022). While we should not extrapolate these results because the roles and responsibilities of interpreters differ significantly to those of learning support assistants, we should caution against considering this relationship as entirely positive.

Peer-Tutoring

Josie and Sarah are friends. They have been for several years now. They know each other well. That's why Ms Patel asked Josie to be a part of the peer-tutoring training programme to support Sarah. The training was fascinating *said Josie, explaining it to Sarah and their other friend Tara.* "I learned some sign language and other hand signals. I learned about how to demonstrate some of the techniques we use in tennis and how to give feedback. We even discussed where I should stand and the importance of Sarah being able to see me at all times. I found it so interesting. I really want to be a PE teacher so I think it will be really useful for that too", *she said.*

Practitioner-based resources provide numerous suggestions about the utility of trained peer tutors in physical education classes for Deaf students (e.g., Davis, 2011; Lieberman & Houston-Wilson, 2009). According to Liberman and Houston-Wilson (2009), it is important to differentiate between peer interaction and peer tutoring because the latter, unlike the former, requires the tutor to receive formal protocol-based training. Peer tutors who have an affinity with the Deaf students are encouraged in several practitioner texts (e.g., Lieberman & Houston-Wilson, 2009; Roth et al., 2016). According to research Lieberman et al. (2000), a properly trained hearing peer tutor can impact positively on skill development and the physical activity level of both themselves and Deaf students because it frees up more time in the lesson. Peer tutoring is also said to allow for individualised instruction, positive reinforcement and regular feedback, all of which improve performance in physical education (Lieberman & Houston-Wilson, 2009; Schultz et al., 2013). There are many different types of peer-tutoring programmes, including unidirectional, bidirectional or reciprocal, class-wide, same-age and cross-age peer tutoring. Please read Liberman and Houston-Wilson (2009) if you are interested in learning more about peer-tutoring programmes but please be aware that this is a practitioner text that lacks empirical support.

While much has been written in practitioner texts about the value of peer-tutoring and buddy systems in physical education (e.g., Davis, 2011; Lieberman & Houston-Wilson, 2009; Roth et al., 2016; Winnick &

Porretta, 2016), most of it lacks empirical support, especially research that is grounded in Deaf students' experiences in physical education specifically. Thus, there are clear (dis)connections between what is suggested for practitioners to do, and empirical support for these suggestions. There is a need for researchers to systematically explore who should be recruited for peer-tutor training, what the training should specifically involve depending on the preferred outcomes (in physical education) and what role(s) peer-tutors should perform during physical education lessons. Here, teacher, peer-tutor and Deaf student perspectives will be key for developing a more rounded and credible knowledge and understanding. Moreover, while there is some research about the influence of peer-tutoring on physical activities levels (e.g., Lieberman et al., 2000), there is an urgent need to explore the impact of these programmes on cognitive development, social and emotional learning and the development of physical skills among both Deaf students and peer-tutor because these too are important outcomes of physical education (Bailey, 2018; Maher & Fitzgerald, 2020). Peer-tutoring is an established approach in physical education that, at present, lacks the evidence-based required to have confidence in its widespread use.

Conclusion

This chapter provided a brief overview of deafness and Deaf children and young people, before exploring, using vignettes and discussions of published literature, strategies that are most frequently promoted and used when teaching physical education to Deaf students. While we hope that this chapter has given you some ideas to consider relating to working with interpreters, teacher positioning during lessons and the use of non-verbal cues and peer-tutoring, we also encourage you to be critical of the research-based supporting these practices. Indeed, the onus here is on teachers to engage in pedagogical experimentation to see what works best for whom in what settings and under what conditions. Reflective diaries, lesson observations and discussions with Deaf students, hearing students, learning support assistants and interpreters can all be used to generate data to help ensure that your teaching of Deaf students is evidence informed.

References

Action on Hearing Loss. (2015). *Hearing matters*. Action on Hearing Loss.
Bailey, R. (2018). Sport, physical education and educational worth. *Educational Review, 70*(1), 51–66. https://doi.org/10.1080/00131911.2018.1403208

Barboza, C. F. S., Campello, A. R., & Castro, H. C. (2015). Sports, physical education, Olympic Games, and Brazil: The deafness that still should be listened. *Creative Education, 6*, 1386–1390. http://doi.org/10.4236/ce.2015.612138

Barnes, C., Mercer, G., & Shakespeare, T. (1999). *Exploring disability: A sociological introduction.* Polity Press.

Bauman, H. (2008). Listening to phonocentrism with Deaf eyes: Derrida's mute philosophy of (sign) language. *Essays in Philosophy, 9*(1), 41–54. https://doi.org/10.5840/eip20089118

Consortium for Research in Deaf Education. (2019). 2019 UK-wide summary CRIDE report on 2018/2019 survey on educational provision for deaf children. Available at: https://www.ndcs.org.uk/media/6550/cride-2019-uk-wide-report-final.pdf

Davis, R. (2011). *Teaching disability sport: A guide for physical educators* (2nd ed.). Human Kinetics.

De Kegel, A., Dhooge, I., Cambier, D., Baetens, T., Palmans, T., & Van Waelvelde, H. (2011). Test–retest reliability of the assessment of postural stability in typically developing children and in hearing impaired children. *Gait & Posture, 33*(4), 679–685. https://doi.org/10.1016/j.gaitpost.2011.02.024

Fiorini, M., & Manzini, E. (2018). Strategies of physical education teachers to promote the participation of students with hearing impairment in classrooms. *Revista Brasileira de Educacao Especial, 24*, 183–198. https://doi.org/10.1590/s1413- 65382418000200003

Friedner, M., & Block, P. (2017). Deaf studies meets autistic studies. *The Senses and Society, 12*(3), 282–300. https://doi.org/10.1080/17458927.2017.1369716

Friedner, M., & Helmreich, S. (2012). Sound studies meets Deaf studies. *The Senses and Society, 7*(1), 72–86. https://doi.org/10.2752/174589312X13173255802120

Goodwin, D., Rossow-Kimball, B., & Connolly, M. (2022). Students' experiences of paraeducator support in inclusive physical education: Helping or hindering? *Sport, Education and Society, 27*(2), 182–195. https://doi.org/10.1080/13573322.2021.1931835

Hodge, S., Lieberman, L., & Murata, N. (2012). *Essentials of teaching physical education: Culture, diversity, and inclusion.* Holcomb Hathaway.

Kim, E., Byrne, B., & Parish, S. (2018). Deaf people and economic well-being: Findings from the Life Opportunities Survey. *Disability & Society, 33*(3), 374–391. https://doi.org/10.1080/09687599.2017.1420631

Lieberman, L. (2016). Hard-of-hearing, deaf, or deafblind. In D. Porretta & J. Winnick (Eds.), *Adapted physical education and sport* (5th ed., pp. 253–271). Human Kinetics.

Lieberman, L., Dunn, J., van der Mars, H., & McCubbin, J. (2000). Peers tutors' effects on activity levels of Deaf students in inclusive elementary physical education. *Adapted Physical Activity Quarterly, 17*, 20–39. https://doi.org/10.1123/apaq.17.1.20

Lieberman, L. J., & Houston-Wilson, C. (2009). *Strategies for inclusion* (2nd ed.). Human Kinetics.

Li, C., Haegele, J., & Wu, L. (2018). Comparing physical activity and sedentary behavior levels between deaf and hearing adolescents. *Disability and Health Journal, 12*(3), 514–518. https://doi.org/10.1016/j.dhjo.2018.12.002

Lobenius-Palmér, K., Sjqvist, B., Hurtig-Wennlof, A., & Lundqvist, L. (2018). Accelerometer-assessed physical activity and sedentary time in youth with disabilities. *Adapted Physical Activity Quarterly, 35*, 1–19. https://doi.org/10.1123/apaq.2015-0065

Luft, P. (2015). Transition services for DHH adolescents and young adults with Disabilities: Challenges and theoretical frameworks. *American Annals of the Deaf, 160*(4), 395–414. https://doi.org/10.1353/aad.2015.0028

Maher, A. (2010). The inclusion of pupils with special educational needs: A study of the formulation and implementation of the National Curriculum Physical Education in Britain. *Sport Science Review, XIX*(1–2), 87–117. http://dx.doi.org/10.2478/v10237-011-0006-y

Maher, A. J. (2020). Disrupting phonocentricism for teaching Deaf pupils: Prospective physical education teachers' learning about visual pedagogies and non-verbal communication. *Physical Education and Sport Pedagogy.* https://doi.org/10.1080/17408989.2020.1806996

Maher, A. J., & Fitzgerald, H. (2020). The culture of special schools: The nature, purpose and value of physical education. *Educational Review* [online first]. https://doi.org/10.1080/00131911.2020.1721437

Majlesi, M., Farahpour, N., Azadian, E., & Amini, M. (2014). The effect of interventional proprioceptive training on static balance and gait in deaf children. *Research in Developmental Disabilities, 35*(12), 3562–3567. https://doi.org/10.1016/j.ridd.2014.09.001

Mourão, C. (2008). Ensinando educação física para surdos: Análise de caso. In *3th Seminário Brasileiro de Estudos Culturais e Educação* (pp. 1–12). Porto Alegre, RS: Plannertec Informática e Sistemas Ltda.

Padden, C., & Humphries., T. (1988). *Deaf in America.* Harvard University Press.

Reich, L., & Lavay, B. (2009). Physical education and sport adaptations for students who are hard of hearing. *Journal of Physical Education, Recreation & Dance, 80*(3), 38–49. https://doi.org/10.1080/07303084.2009.10598295

Rine, R., Cornwall, G., Can, K., Locascio, C., O'hare, T., Robinson, E., et al. (2000). Evidence of progressive delay of motor development in children with sensorineural hearing loss and concurrent vestibular dysfunction. *Perceptual and Motor Skills, 90*(3), 1101–1112. https://doi.org/10.2466%2Fpms.2000.90.3c.1101

Roth, K., Zittel, L., Pyfer, J., & Auxter, D. (2016). *Principles and methods of adapted physical education and recreation* (12th ed.). McGraw-Hill.

Schultz, J., Lieberman, L., Ellis, M., & Hilgenbrinck, L. (2013). Ensuring the success of Deaf students in inclusive physical education. *Journal of Physical Education, Recreation & Dance, 84*(5), 51–56. https://doi.org/10.1080/07303084.2013.779535

Winnick, J., & Porretta, D. (Eds.). (2016). *Adapted physical education and sport* (6th ed.). Human Kinetics.

5 Teaching Students Experiencing Cognitive and Learning Difficulties in Physical Education

Background and Context

Cognitive and learning difficulties is an umbrella term used in this book to describe students who experience generalised movement difficulties and who are not recognised as physically disabled individuals or as being clumsy or experiencing developmental coordination disorder (Vickerman & Maher, 2019). Internationally, cognitive and learning difficulties are conceptualised and defined in several different ways, and, as such, there is some difficulty in gaining an understanding of precise estimates of the number of students that may experience these difficulties. For example, in the United Kingdom, the Office for Health Improvement and Disparities (2022) suggests that approximately 296,000 pupils in schools experience *learning difficulties*, which includes 250,000 with moderate learning difficulties, about 32,000 with severe learning difficulties and about 11,000 with severe learning difficulties. In the United States, though, cognitive and learning difficulties tend to be conceptualised using labels such as *intellectual disabilities or cognitive impairments* and *specific learning disabilities*. Within the United States, recent estimates suggest that just under 1% of the student population in public schools experience intellectual disabilities or cognitive impairments, whereas approximately 14% have been identified as experiencing learning disabilities (National Center for Education Statistics, 2020). In addition, many estimates internationally are diagnosis specific, such as estimated rates of approximately 7.2% of children being diagnosed with attention deficit/hyperactivity disorder, the most prevalent learning disability, worldwide (CHADD, 2019). In most regions, though, it is clear that students experiencing cognitive and learning difficulties make up a substantial percentage of the school population, generally considered among the largest, if not the largest, disability groups serviced within integrated mainstream schools.

DOI: 10.4324/9781003176282-5

For us, it is important to note that students experiencing cognitive and learning difficulties are often identified as exhibiting poor motor skill development and low levels of physical activity (Bishop & Pangelinan, 2018; Harvey et al., 2007; Wouters et al., 2019). These difficulties may translate into poor experiences within integrated physical education contexts, where students with cognitive and learning difficulties have reporting feeling discriminated against by their peers and teachers (Coates, 2011; Fitzgerald, 2005, 2012; Harvey et al., 2014). However, movement-related difficulties are not inexplicably linked to cognitive and learning difficulties, and some children, particularly those with moderate cognitive or learning difficulties, will perform well and perhaps excel within physical activity environments, like physical education (Vickerman & Maher, 2019).

Overview of Cognitive and Learning Difficulties

As described in the prior section, cognitive and learning difficulties appear to be understood differently depending on context. In the United Kingdom, the term *cognitive and learning difficulties* is typically used to describe students who experience generalised movement difficulties (Vickerman & Maher, 2019). As such, understandings of learning difficulties in the United Kingdom appear to be heavily centred on the students' abilities and capabilities within schools and classrooms, rather than specific diagnoses. Elsewhere, such as the United States, phrases such as *intellectual disabilities* or *cognitive impairment* tend to be used to describe students who experience cognitive limitations as well as functional limitations in daily living, communication or social skills, who are then grouped by IQ (Cavanaugh & Hilgenbrink, 2021). In addition, *specific learning disabilities* is also commonly used in the United States and elsewhere to describe students who have trouble learning that is generally associated with a neurological condition (e.g., attention deficit/hyperactivity disorder) (Lavay & Bittner, 2021). In the United States, a heavy emphasis is placed on diagnosis, and special education services within schools are gatekept to only those who provide documented diagnoses, usually diagnoses that are aligned with federal educational legislation.

Aim and Purpose

The aim of this chapter is to explore and critique strategies that are discussed in academic literature to teach students who experience cognitive or learning difficulties in physical education. Like other chapters within this text, particular attention will be paid to exploring strategies that are discussed for use in integrated physical education contexts, clearly prioritising these settings over other educational spaces. While this prioritisation is not in line with our personal or professional beliefs, we believe it is reflective of the field as a whole, and therefore critical when reflecting about scholarship and practice. To guide our critique, brief non-fiction stories are provided that depict experiences of Sonny, a student who experiences a cognitive or learning difficulty, and his experiences with strategies that are commonly presented when teaching students like him. Unlike other chapters, we are purposely ambiguous here when describing characteristics that might describe Sonny's cognitive or learning difficulty, as we believe that this is aligned with the little complete or accurate information that physical educators typically receive when meeting with students experiencing these difficulties. Following each story, we discuss and critique each of the strategies used within the story while centring the extant literature. Particular focus within the literature is placed on studies that centre on the voices of students experiencing cognitive and learning difficulties within schools.

Cooperative Teaching/Learning Activities

Sonny struggles sometimes during competitive activities, and this appears to be particularly true during volleyball class sessions. While he understands where to stand during volleyball, as well as many of the rules within volleyball, such as needing to hit the ball three times prior to sending it over the net, he's never felt very good about his ability to execute the skills when the competition is on. Making matters worse, he appears to be hurting his team, and he feels that his teammates often grow frustrated with him during volleyball. For Sonny, it appears that sitting out of volleyball may be a more suitable option for him. Mrs Sparkles knows this, based on Sonny's past behaviour and some conversations they've had, and she's devised a plan. As Sonny and his classmates enter the sports hall for volleyball, they learn that they are playing a different game this year. It looks kinda like volleyball, but it isn't. Instead of playing against other teams, they are working together with the other team to see how many times they can hit the ball over the net without it hitting the ground. Sonny feels encouraged, cautiously, and ready to give this new game a chance.

Cooperative teaching and learning activities are an important place to begin this section, since it is the most commonly discussed pedagogical recommendation in practice-based articles and book chapters focused on students experiencing cognitive and learning difficulties (e.g., Grenier & Yeaton, 2019; Higgins et al., 2018; Mach, 2000). Cooperative teaching and learning activities represent a pivot away from competitive games where students, rather, engage in co-operative, team building activities (Grenier & Yeaton, 2019; Mach, 2000). According to Dyson and Grineski (2001), cooperative learning is defined 'as small-group instruction and practice that uses positive student interactions as a means of achieving instructional goals' (p. 28). This approach is characterised using small, cooperative activities that require students to work together to meet a common goal and can include a variety of structures, such as *think-share-perform*, *pairs-check-perform* and *jigsaw perform* (Dyson & Grineski, 2001; Orlick 2006). According to Johnson and colleagues (2013), there are five fundamental elements of cooperative learning, positive interdependence, promotive interaction, individual responsibility, group processing and interpersonal skills. This approach has been promoted as a way to promote student interpersonal skills while combining aspects of social and academic learning (Casey & Goodyear, 2015; Dyson & Grineski, 2001). To date, there is a considerable body of research that suggests that the use of cooperative learning in physical education can help with achieving gains in physical, cognitive, social and affective domains (Bores-Garcia et al., 2021; Casey & Goodyear, 2015) among nondisabled students.

While the research body is substantial, and growing, that explores cooperative learning in physical education among nondisabled students, research in this area of inquiry has largely ignored disabled students, including those experiencing cognitive or learning difficulties. This point was recently discussed by Block and colleagues (2021), who identified that while curricular models like cooperative learning have been developed, tested and refined, research on these models has largely been conducted without disabled students in mind. This is despite several practice-based papers highlighting the utility of cooperative learning for students experiencing cognitive or learning difficulties (Grenier et al., 2005; Grenier & Yeaton, 2019; Mach, 2000). Highlighting this, among two systematic reviews published recently by Bores-Garcia and colleagues (2021) and Casey and Goodyear (2015), just one study by Andre et al. (2011) was identified as centring on disabled students. This study, however, was concerned more so with whether cooperative learning tasks could demonstrate utility in helping nondisabled students have more favourable perspectives towards students experiencing cognitive and learning difficulties (Andre et al., 2011), and less so on the experiences of or educational benefits for disabled students. Importantly, though, a follow-up study by the same authorship team did provide some support for cooperative learning for students who experience cognitive or learning difficulties. Indeed, those who participated in *risky* activities within a cooperative learning context were identified as experiencing significantly more acceptance than those in a non-risk control group (Andre et al., 2013).

Perhaps scholars and practitioners should look outside of physical education for further support for the use of cooperative learning, which appears available in general education contexts (Sencibaugh & Sencibaugh, 2016), however this would ignore the unique educational context, curricula and pedagogies that exist within physical education spaces. As such, and despite the potential promise cooperative learning may have for engaging students experiencing cognitive and learning difficulties in meaningful physical education experiences, little research outside of the studies by Andre and colleagues (2011, 2013) is available to support the utility of cooperative learning in this context. This includes a clear lack of scholarship that has engaged students experiencing cognitive and learning difficulties in conversations about their views of these cooperative educational experiences.

Micro-Teaching Tips

Within P.E., Sonny notices that Mrs Sparkles has been treating him a bit differently than other kids since she learned that he experiences a cognitive or learning difficulty. She now asks Sonny to remain close to her while she provides instruction, and for him to repeat instructions back to her after she explains tasks to his group. She also appears to position herself directly in front of Sonny when providing instructions to the class, sometimes with visual cards. While Sonny doesn't feel any particular way about these behaviours, they are quite different than how Mrs Sparkles interacts with the other students, and Sonny is noticing that other students see this seemingly preferential treatment as well. He wonders what the repercussions might be…

The micro-teaching tips that are presented in the non-fiction narrative above, such as keeping students close to the instructor, using visuals to support instruction and asking students to repeat directions to determine comprehension, are commonly explicated recommendations in book chapters and practice-based articles (Mach, 2000; Petersen et al., 2004; Stanton-Nichols & Block, 2016). According to Petersen and colleagues (2004), using teaching tips like these can be helpful with ensuring that students experiencing a variety of cognitive or learning difficulties can be successful within the integrated physical education context. For Stanton-Nichols and Block (2016), some of these practices, which are generally conceptualised as *simplifying* within a recommendation for specific instructional modifications, are aligned with easily implemented practices that are generally considered as good teaching. Others have pointed towards some of these strategies, such as positioning students at the front of a class, as being helpful for reducing distraction and enhancing attentiveness (Higgins et al., 2018). As such, it appears that these practices are generally considered to be obvious solutions or best practices that could, and perhaps should, be implemented regularly within integrated physical education when engaging with students with cognitive or learning difficulties.

Like many other areas, there is a clear (dis)connection between these explicated best practices and empirical support for them. That is, while perhaps these teaching behaviours represent what might be considered *good teaching*, they are not necessarily empirically supported, particularly for students experiencing cognitive or learning difficulties within integrated physical education contexts. There may also be some repercussions of these behaviours that may need to be considered. First, close proximity to adult stakeholders within physical education settings has been shown to drive a wedge between disabled and nondisabled students by unintentionally dissuading peers from communicating and interacting with disabled students during class (Haegele et al., 2017). As such, despite nondisabled and disabled students engaging in activities within the same setting, the close proximity of adults may restrict peer-to-peer contact, thus reducing the likelihood of social interactions. Second, engaging directly, and constantly, with students experiencing cognitive and learning difficulties can place additional attention, or spotlight, on those students. When teachers place a spotlight on disabled students, intentionally or unintentionally, through providing special attention or individualised instruction, they are communicating to peers, perhaps implicitly, that there is something unique about the individual student, and therefore may be taking away a student's option to, or not to, disclose their impairment to their classmates (Fitzgerald, 2005; Haegele et al., 2017). This is problematic, as impairment disclosure is a personal decision, one that is particularly relevant among students experiencing hidden disabilities, and can lead to further social repercussions, such as social isolation or marginalisation from peers during integrated physical education classes (Fitzgerald, 2005; Moola et al., 2011). This challenge is hinted at towards the end of Sonny's narrative, where he questions what repercussions might exist from other students noticing his special treatment.

Class Organisation

In addition to realising that Mrs Sparkles may be treating him differently than before, as well as differently from his peers, Sonny has also realised that some of the procedures and organisation in physical education has changed recently. He's noticed that Mrs Sparkles is spending more time setting clear boundaries with cones throughout the gym, and is using colour organised activities with matching balls, cones and spots. With the current fitness unit, Sonny is also participating in far more activities within small groups in stations, where he spends a minute or two in a station participating in a specific activity before moving on. There's even a timer that goes off at the end of the two minutes, to remind the entire class to leave. Sonny's been enjoying stations so far, as he's with his friends at each station, and he has a good idea of what to do and there are even small pictures at each station for reminders. Mrs Sparkles appears a bit more relaxed as well, perhaps because she doesn't have to spend the entire class instructing and can come around and chat with her students throughout class.

Like the other pedagogical recommendations in this chapter, tips for class organisation are present throughout most practice-based papers (e.g., Higgins et al., 2018; Mulrine & Flores-Marti, 2014) and book chapters (Cavanaugh & Hilgenbrink, 2021) focused on students with cognitive or learning difficulties. According to Higgins and colleagues (2018), class organisation 'helps make the physical education environment more pleasant' and may include tasks like setting clear boundaries and barriers using spots, cones or paint. Further, they suggest that physical education environments may even include areas of seclusion within the integrated setting to help reduce overstimulation, if needed (Higgins et al., 2018). Most common among recommendations, though, might be the utilisation of learning stations, as described by Sonny, which divide the physical education space into multiple small areas and present a variety of different related activities at the stations for students to engage in (Cavanaugh & Hilgenbrink, 2021; Haegele & Park, 2016). Station teaching, according to Siedentop and Tannehill (2000), includes organising the learning environment so that different students can engage in different learning tasks at the same time. Generally, stations can focus on a specific theme, such as physical fitness or a specific sport, and each includes a different aspect of that sport to practice. Suggested benefits of learning stations include opportunities to engage in targeted practice with specific aspects of activities for more trials (Haegele & Park, 2016), and to work within smaller groups while integrating students into large classes (Cavanaugh & Hilgenbrink, 2021; Siedentop & Tannehill, 2000).

Like other areas described in this chapter, little focused empirical research connects class organisation strategies explicated in practice-based resources to data shared through empirical studies in physical education contexts that focus on students experiencing cognitive or learning difficulties. In many instances within each of these practice-based resources, it appears that conceptual or theoretical support (in the form of citations and references) for pedagogical suggestions are informed or influenced by prior practice-based papers. That is, rather than rooting these suggestions in data-based studies that have examined the efficacy of these pedagogical suggestions, a problematic cycle appears to have emerged where practices are recommended based on prior recommended practices and so on. As such, like other sections, a (dis)connection between practice and scholarship is evident. This is not to question existing data supporting benefits associated with station work or class organisation in other settings or contexts, as well as in physical education environments for nondisabled students. However, little, to our knowledge, supports these recommendations, outside of perhaps common-sense ideologies, for students experiencing cognitive or learning difficulties.

Conclusion

This chapter provides a brief overview of cognitive and learning difficulties before exploring strategies most frequently described for educating students experiencing cognitive and learning difficulties within integrated physical education contexts. While writing this particular chapter, we found that very little scholarship, either presenting best practice strategies or empirical research to support these strategies, exists to support the education of students experiencing cognitive or learning difficulties in physical education. Even categorical textbooks that include book chapters in this area seem to provide general teaching tips rather than pedagogical strategies specifically designed and tested for this population. This may not be surprising, as some have suggested that little changes should be made to integrated environments for educating those experiencing cognitive and learning disabilities, particularly those mild in nature. This lack of practical and empirical scholarship makes recommendations for teaching practices challenging at best, which is important for us to consider when discussing and describing how best to teach students experiencing cognitive and learning difficulties in physical education. Perhaps this is an opportunity for future work, particularly research that centres the voices of those experiencing cognitive and learning difficulties like those from Fitzgerald (2005, 2007) and Harvey and colleagues (2014), to play a significant role in constructing recommended teaching practices as well as problematising some of the few strategies currently depicted in textbook chapters and elsewhere. As such, we take this opportunity to further recommend work that engages with students experiencing cognitive and learning difficulties to help co-construct pedagogical practices that could support meaningful experiences in integrated physical education contexts.

References

Andre, A., Deneuve, P., & Louvet, B. (2011). Cooperative learning in physical education and acceptance of students with learning disabilities. *Journal of Applied Sport Psychology, 23*(4), 474–485. https://doi.org/10.1080/10413200.2011.580826

Andre, A., Louvet, B., & Deneuve, P. (2013). Cooperative group, risk-taking and inclusion of pupils with learning disabilities in physical education. *British Educational Research Journal, 39*(4), 677–693. https://doi.org/10.1080/01411926.2012.674102

Block, M. E., Haegele, J. A., Kelly, L., & Obrusnikova, I. (2021). Exploring future research in adapted physical education. *Research Quarterly for Exercise & Sport, 92*(3), 429–442. https://doi.org/10.1080/02701367.2020.1741500

Bishop, J. C., & Pangelinan, M. (2018). Motor skills intervention research of children with disabilities. *Research in Developmental Disabilities, 74*, 14–30. https://doi.org/10.1080/02701367.2020.1741500

Bores-Garcia, D., Hortiguela-Alcala, D., Fernandez-Rio, F., Gonzalez-Calvo, G., & Barba-Martin, R. (2021). Research on cooperative learning in physical education: Systematic review of the last five years. *Research Quarterly for Exercise & Sport, 92*(1), 146–155. https://doi.org/10.1080/02701367.2020.1719276

Casey, A., & Goodyear, V. A. (2015). Can cooperative learning achieve the four learning outcomes of physical education? A review of literature. *Quest, 67*(1), 56–72. https://doi.org/10.1080/00336297.2014.984733

Cavanaugh, L. K., & Hilgenbrink, L. C. (2021). Intellectual disabilities. In J. P. Winnick & D. L. Porretta (Eds.), *Adapted physical education and sport* (7th ed., pp. 151–172). Human Kinetics.

Children and Adults with Attention Deficit/Hyperactivity Disorder (CHADD). (2019). *ADHD fact sheets & infographics*. https://chadd.org/understanding-adhd/adhd-fact-sheets/

Coates, J. (2011). Physically fit or physically literate? How children with special educational needs understand physical education. *European Physical Education Review, 17*(2), 167–181. https://doi.org/10.1177/1356336X11413183

Dyson, B., & Grineski, S. (2001). Using cooperative learning structures in physical education. *Journal of Physical Education, Recreation & Dance, 72*(2), 28–31. https://doi.org/10.1080/07303084.2001.10605831

Fitzgerald, H. (2005). Still feeling like a spare piece of luggage? Embodied experiences of (dis)ability in physical education and school sport. *Physical Education & Sport Pedagogy, 10*(1), 41–59. https://doi.org/10.1080/1740898042000334908

Fitzgerald. H. (2007). Dramatizing physical education: Using drama in research. *British Journal of Learning Disabilities, 35*(4), 253–260. https://doi.org/10.1111/j.1468-3156.2007.00471.x

Fitzgerald, H. (2012). 'Drawing' on disabled students' experiences of physical education and stakeholder responses. *Sport, Education, & Society, 17*, 443–462. https://doi.org/10.1080/13573322.2011.609290

Grenier, M., Dyson, B., & Yeaton, P. (2005). Cooperative learning that includes students with disabilities. *Journal of Physical Education, Recreation, & Dance, 76*(6), 29–35. https://doi.org/10.1080/07303084.2005.10608264

Grenier, M., & Yeaton, P. (2019). Social thinking skills and cooperative learning for students with autism. *Journal of Physical Education, Recreation, & Dance, 90*(3), 18–21. http://doi.org/10.1080/07303084.2019.1559675

Haegele, J. A., & Park, S. Y. (2016). Utilizing generalization tactics to promote leisure-time physical activity for students with intellectual impairments. *Strategies, 29*(4), 19–23. https://doi.org/10.1080/08924562.2016.1181592

Haegele, J. A., Sato, T., Zhu, X., & Kirk, T. N. (2017). Paraeducator support in integrated physical education as reflected by adults with visual impairments. *Adapted Physical Activity Quarterly, 36*(1), 91–108. https://doi.org/10.1123/apaq.2018-0063

Harvey, W. J., Reid, G., Grizenko, N., Mbekou, V., Ter-Stepanian, M., & Joober, R. (2007). Fundamental movement skills and children with attention-deficit hyperactivity disorder: Peer comparisons and stimulant effects. *Journal of Abnormal Child Psychology, 35*, 871–882. https://doi.org/10.1007/s10802-007-9140-5

Harvey, W. J., Wilkinson, S., Presse, C., Joober, R., & Grizenko, N. (2014). Children say the darndest things: Physical activity and children with attention-deficit hyperactivity disorder. *Physical Education & Sport Pedagogy, 19*(2), 205–220. https://doi.org/10.1080/17408989.2012.754000

Higgins, A. K., Sluder, B., Richards, J. M., & Buchanan, A. (2018). A new and improved physical education setting for children with ADHD. *Strategies, 31*(4), 26–32. https://doi.org/10.1080/08924562.2018.1465869

Johnson, D. W., Johnson, R. T., & Holubec, E. J. (2013). *Cooperation in the classroom* (9th ed.). Interaction Book Company.

Lavay, B. W., & Bittner, M. D. (2021). Specific learning disabilities. In J. P. Winnick & D. L. Porretta (Eds.), *Adapted physical education and sport* (7th ed., pp. 213–232). Human Kinetics.

Mach, M. M. (2000). Teaching and coaching students with learning disabilities and attentional deficits. *Strategies, 13*(4), 12–31. https://doi.org/10.1080/08924562.2000.11000322

Moola, F., Fusco, C., & Kirsh, J. A. (2011). 'What I wish you knew': Social barriers toward physical activity in youth with congenital heart disease (CHD). *Adapted Physical Activity Quarterly, 28*(1), 56–77. https://doi.org/10.1123/apaq.28.1.56

Mulrine, C., & Flores-Marti, I. (2014). Practical strategies for teaching students with attention-deficit hyperactive disorder in general physical education classrooms. *Strategies, 27*(1), 26–31. https://doi.org/10.1080/08924562.2014.859004

National Center for Educational Statistics (NCES). (2020). *Fast facts: Students with disabilities.* http://nces.ed.gov/fastfacts/display.asp?id=64

Office for Health Improvement and Disparities. (2022). *Learning disability profiles.* https://fingertips.phe.org.uk/profile/learning-disabilities/data#page/1/gid/1938132702/ati/15/iid/92127/age/217/sex/4/cat/-1/ctp/-1/yrr/1/cid/4/tbm/1

Orlick, T. (2006). *Cooperative games and sport: Joyful activities for everyone.* Human Kinetics.

Petersen, S. C., Grosshans, J., & Kiger, M. (2004). Identifying and teaching children with learning disabilities in general physical education. *Journal of Physical Education, Recreation, & Dance, 75*(6), 18–20. https://doi.org/10.1080/07303084.2004.10607250

Sencibaugh, J. M., & Sencibaugh, A. M. (2016). An analysis of cooperative learning approaches for students with learning disabilities. *Education, 136*(3), 356–364.

Siedentop, D., & Tannehill, D. (2000). *Developing teaching skills in physical education.* McGraw-Hill.

Stanton-Nichols, K., & Block, M. E. (2016). Intellectual disabilities. In M. E. Block (Ed.), *A teacher's guide to adapted physical education* (4th ed.). Brookes.

Vickerman, P., & Maher, A. (2019). *Teaching physical education to children with special educational needs and disabilities* (2nd ed.). Routledge.

Wouters, M., Evenhuis, H. M., & Hilgenkamp, T. I. (2019). Physical activity levels of children and adolescents with moderate-to-severe intellectual disability. *Journal of Applied Research in Intellectual Disabilities, 32*(1), 131–142. https://doi.org/10.1111/jar.12515

6 Teaching Physically Disabled Students in Physical Education

Background and Context

According to the United Kingdom's Equality Act 2010, physical disability refers to a limitation to a person's physical functioning, mobility, dexterity or stamina that has a substantial, long-term influence on their ability to perform everyday activities (Government Equalities Office, 2022). From 2019 to 2020 in the United Kingdom, a mobility impairment was the most prevalent type of physical disability, reported by 49% (i.e., 7 million) of all disabled people. When it comes to children and young people in the United Kingdom, the Family Resource Survey suggests that 19% of disabled children reported mobility impairment (Department for Work and Pensions, 2021). Of the 61 million people in the United States with a disability, accounting for 21% of the population, 13.7% reported as having a mobility impairment (CDC, 2022). Accordingly, the US Census Bureau (2019) suggests that 4.3% of all people under the age of 18 living in the United States are disabled individuals, with 0.7 of those experiencing what is termed ambulatory disability. Given the link between physical disability, movement, dexterity and stamina, it is perhaps unsurprising that research suggests that disabled children and young people are likely to be less physically active when compared to their nondisabled peers (Shields et al., 2012). A systematic review of literature conducted by Shields and colleagues (2012) attributed this disparity to adults lacking appropriate knowledge, skills and experience to provide appropriate opportunities; negative attitudes about disability; cost; a lack of transport, programmes and staff capacity; inadequate facilities; parental behaviours; and child preferences. In that regard, it was found that the physically disabled child's desire to be active and practise skills were tied to a number of different factors, such as the involvement of peers, family support, accessible facilities,

DOI: 10.4324/9781003176282–6

proximity of location, better opportunities, skilled staff and information (Shields et al., 2012).

Overview of Disability

Physical disability can be invisible (e.g., osteogenesis imperfecta – brittle bones) or visible (e.g., spina bifida), sometimes requiring the use of assistive equipment to facilitate mobility, such as a wheelchair. Like many of the so-called categories of disability and additional learning needs covered in this book, a wide variety of children and young people fall into established definitions of physical disability. Rather than focusing on specific categories or physical manifestations of disability, this chapter covers those children and young people who use a wheelchair to facilitate mobility. Moreover, instead of focusing on physical conditions and impairments of the body as a source of the *problem*, we are more concerned about the ways in which the attitudes and behaviours of nondisabled people, such as teachers and teaching assistants, together with the social setting and physical environments of schools, can create barriers to physically disabled students who use wheelchairs having meaningful experiences of physical education. This perspective is in keeping with social, cultural and relational considerations of disability that move beyond centring the physically disabled body as the problem (Oliver, 2013). As such, and for consistency throughout this book, we use the identity-first language of *physically disabled students*, rather than students with physical disabilities.

Aim and Purpose

The aim of this chapter is to critique the strategies discussed and promoted in academic literature and used to teach and support physically disabled students who are wheelchair users in physical education. To do this, creative non-fiction accounts, which centre on Michael, a pupil who experiences cerebral palsy and who uses a wheelchair for mobility, and Mr Stanton, his physical education teacher, are provided relating to experiences in a mainstream, integrated physical education class. The strategies used in these accounts, which are commonly presented in best practice papers and taught on pre-service teacher training courses, are then discussed in relation to the academic literature supporting them before the evidence-base is critiqued. The chapter ends with practical suggestions for teachers working with physically disabled students, together with recommendations for future research. We hope that this approach supports teachers and other practitioners to make evidence informed decisions when working with physically disabled student wheelchair users. This aligns with our goal of encouraging schools to be more research engaged and supporting teachers as researchers.

Universal Design for Learning

Mr Stanton is planning his lesson carefully. He rarely finds time to plan properly with all his other work responsibilities but has managed to dedicate an hour during a free period. He has locked himself away in a classroom, so no one disturbs him. He needs to get this right, especially after the last lesson. That didn't go so well. Michael seemed to enjoy the lesson, but Mr Stanton can't help but feel that he let himself, and Michael, down. Mr Stanton has never taught a physically disabled student before, or at least one that uses a wheelchair, so he searched the internet to find some tips. It was here that he came across universal design for learning and its principles of representation, actions and expressions and engagement. He starts by thinking about representation. He is teaching dribbling and passing in handball tomorrow and plans to use a few forms of representation when instructing to see what works best for Michael: verbal instruction, notes on the whiteboard, videos and handouts. He also plans to use his tried and tested demonstrations but is unsure how useful they will be for a physical disabled student or wheelchair user. Next, he thinks about actions and expressions – or, in his own language – assessment and evaluations. That's easy, Mr Stanton thinks. I'll ask questions to probe knowledge. I'll also observe and ask students to demonstrate the dribble and pass. Mr Stanton pauses. He ponders. What does a dribble and pass look like for Michael? What are the key teaching points? Back to the internet. I wish I had more time to plan for this, thinks Mr Stanton. Finally, he thinks about engagement. He thinks about what he can do to engage Michael and other students during the lesson. He thinks about how he can give Michael some ownership over his learning. He plans for Michael to decide what equipment he wants to use, the different dribbling techniques he wants to experiment with and the distance, force, and trajectory of the passes he uses. That should get him involved. Moreover, it will help me learn about what Michael can do, thinks Mr Stanton.

The parameter of a discussion about planning for the education of disabled students in integrated physical education are wide. Therefore, we narrow our focus to explore universal design for learning because it is often advocated by academics and used by practitioners in physical education. According to Porretta (2011), universal design for learning can be used to ensure that physically disabled students are included in physical education. Universal design for learning has been described by Lieberman and Houston-Wilson (2018) as a concept, set of principles and/or a framework that supports accessibility for the widest possible range of students. For Kennedy and Yun (2019), this relates specifically to building modifications and scaffolding into lesson planning. According to Lieberman and colleagues (2008), a significant difference in universal design for learning when compared to other approaches is that modifications are embedded in the planning process as an option to be used during the taught session, rather than being an afterthought. In this respect, multiple means of representation, actions and expressions and engagement need to be carefully considered from the very beginning of curriculum and activity planning (van Munster et al., 2019).

Representation refers to how the learning content and materials are represented. Here, a key focus is on presenting materials through multiple sources so that it aligns with different learning preferences (van Munster et al., 2019). Examples include demonstrations, verbal instruction, videos, animations, handouts, notes on whiteboard, diagrams and graphics. To this, Lieberman and Houston-Wilson (2018) add teaching assistants and peer buddies. Actions and expressions relate to how learners express what they have learned. According to CAST (2018), a US organisation that created universal design for learning guidelines, multiple means of action and expression in a lesson is the assessment and evaluation component where students demonstrate their content knowledge and skill. A practitioner-based article published by Gilbert (2019) outlines some of the ways in which universal design for learning can be embedded into so-called *inclusive* physical education. Examples include written tasks, presentations, video tasks, quizzes and so on. Engagement refers to how (well) the learners connect with the learning content and how motivated they are to take part in learning. In this instance, teachers should consider how they create a motivational climate to ensure that all learners are engaged. Both Gilbert (2019) and Lieberman and Houston-Wilson (2018) advocate for a learner centred approach and student choice in relation to equipment selection, force and distance, task variation and pace of progression.

A systematic review of literature conducted in 2017 (Ok et al., 2017), and special issue of *Remedial and Special Education* published in 2020 (King-Sears, 2020), suggest that the universal design for learning framework applied in primary and secondary schools has shown promise for guiding students to achieved desired learning outcomes in both mainstream and special school settings. However, while there is reasonable evidence supporting the use of universal design for learning by teachers in schools, hardly any of the research conducted to date has focused on disabled students or those with additional learning needs in physical education. Indeed, the majority of published literature relating to universal design for learning in physical education is comprised of practitioner-based articles (e.g., Brian et al., 2017; Gilbert, 2019; Grenier et al., 2017; Kennedy & Yun, 2019; Lieberman & Grenier, 2019; Lieberman et al., 2008) and textbooks (e.g., Lieberman et al., 2020), which according to van Munster and colleagues (2019) 'merely cite examples rather than present data or scientific evidence recommending this model as an approach to including disabled students in the context of physical education' (p. 361). Thus, we agree with Lieberman and colleagues' (2020) claim that 'UDL's effectiveness in physical education has yet to be extensively studied' (p. 9). Indeed, the lack of evidence to support universal design for learning in physical education has been discussed by several scholars (e.g., Block et al., 2021; Hutzler, 2020) who have also noted that, while the concept of universal design for learning may have merit, we know little from an empirical standpoint about its application.

Considering the notable lack of research-informed evidence supporting the use of universal design for learning in physical education, we draw attention to Block and colleagues' (2021) recommendations for future areas of inquiry to increase our confidence in using universal design for learning. These recommendations include examining: what physical educators know about universal design for learning and reasons why they are, or are not, implementing this strategy in their classes; how professional preparation programs are educating pre-service teachers about universal design for learning; and, disabled and nondisabled students' beliefs about and experiences of universal design for learning in physical education in terms of creating an environment that meets the needs of all.

Differentiated Instruction

Mr Stanton has spent time carefully planning today's physical education lesson. He wants to ensure that Michael can achieve the same learning outcomes as his peers during the tennis lesson. The focus of today's lesson is serving. When they arrive at the local tennis club, Mr Stanton carefully explains and then demonstrates the tennis serve. Then, he groups students with a variety of different ability levels together based on his observations during last week's lesson, before sending them over to a court each to practice. Keeping Michael behind, Mr Stanton shows him a video he found on the internet of a wheelchair tennis player serving during a game. He pauses the video a few times to explain the key technical points that, again, he read on the internet. This has become a familiar routine for Michael, who very soon after joins his group and waits a short time for his turn to practice his serve. Mr Stanton then proceeds to walk around the tennis courts, observing the students, occasionally offers words of wisdom and encouragement as he goes. After a short while, he notices that Michael seems to have mastered the technique. Therefore, he places hoops of different sizes in different places in the serving area to challenge Michael to improve his serving accuracy. Michael appreciates this additional challenge and immediately aims for the smallest hoop.

According to Metzler and Colquitt (2021), traditional forms of pedagogy are based on a *one-size fits all* model to teaching disabled and nondisabled students. The same, it should be noted, has been said about curriculum decisions and assessment arrangements (Maher & Fitzgerald, 2020). Differentiated instruction was developed to move away from universal approaches to teaching and learning by focusing on the individual needs and abilities of students (Tomlinson, 1995, 2014). More specifically, Jarvis and colleagues (2017) contend that teachers need to move beyond delivering content on the assumption that all students of a similar chronological age have the same background knowledge, skill level, interests and preferences. Tomlinson and Imbeau (2010) suggest that differentiated instruction should be considered as a teaching philosophy that requires teachers to utilise pedagogical content knowledge to support the learning and development of diverse learners. Generally, writing and research relating to differentiated instruction focuses on four aspects of teaching and learning: content, process, products and learning environment.

According to Colquitt et al. (2017), *content* is not about curriculum decisions but, rather, refers to affective, cognitive and psychomotor learning, and thus can be demonstrated through student attitudes, understanding and skills. Hence, the purpose here is not to change the content but rather for teachers to offer multiple ways for physically disabled students to achieve the desired learning outcomes of a lesson or unit. Santangelo and Tomlinson (2012) argue that the grouping of students in physical education is one way that teachers can differentiate *process* activities. Grouping in relation to (perceptions of) ability, interests, heterogeneousness and learning profiles is often used in physical education. Despite this, it is important to caution that grouping activities, if not carefully considered by teachers, can contribute towards the marginalisation of disabled students (Maher et al., 2021) and thus impact negatively on their feelings of belonging (Haegele &

Maher, 2022) in physical education. *Products* evidence student learning. They can include formative and summative assessment (Colquitt et al., 2017). Differentiated assessments, according to Colquitt et al. (2017), should be flexible, authentic and tied to the needs, capabilities, interests and learning targets of disabled learners. While this may not be an easy task for teachers, Metzler and Colquitt (2021) remind us that teacher assessments are simply tools that serve to produce representations of student learning in a unit. Last, but by no means least, differentiated instruction requires teachers to consider and differentiate the physical environment, social setting and emotional climate where interactions and learning take place. In this respect, there should be a focus on the accessibility of the physical space, positive interactions and relationships among disabled and nondisabled students based on collaboration and the lesson should be challenging and motivating for all students (Colquitt et al., 2017; van Munster et al., 2019).

In research terms, differentiated instruction in physical education has received very little attention. Indeed, while much has been written about it in practitioner-based journals (e.g., Colquitt et al., 2017; Jarvis et al., 2017) and textbooks (e.g., Block, 2016; Lieberman & Houston-Wilson, 2018; Winnick & Porretta, 2017), the focus has primarily been on explaining how to use differentiated instruction in physical education rather than providing a research base to justify its use. Of important note, this includes a lack of research exploring differentiated instruction from those who embody experiences in differentiated settings and activities, the physically disabled students' themselves. Saying that, some attempt has been made to gather empirical evidence relating to differentiated instruction. For instance, van Munster and colleagues (2019) conducted one of very few studies that has gathered primary data relating to the use of differentiated instruction in physical education. For this, the researchers observed and interviewed physical education teachers and disabled students, including some physically disabled students, to explore the utility of differentiated instruction and universal design for learning in physical education. According to van Munster and colleagues (2019), both universal design for learning and differentiated instruction offer effective and appropriate resources to accommodate disabled students in physical education classes, provided that the decision between using one or the other is based on prior analysis of the learning context. Importantly, though, learning was not formally evaluated in this study, which adds some questions to those assertions.

Given this notable dearth of research relating to differentiated instruction, we suggest that future research needs to focus on disabled learners' experiences of differentiated instruction. Indeed, given claims that one size *does not* fit all, the appropriateness of differentiated instruction needs to be explored from the perspective of a wide range of disabled learners. While disability should not be considered a homogenous category or marker of identity, the same being said about physical disability, Deafness, blindness and so on, the needs and capabilities of learners who are attributed to these categories and identities will be diverse. Therefore, there is a need to explore how differentiated instruction is experienced by all the groups of students outlined in this book. Moreover, if experiences within differentiated instruction are viewed favourably by disabled students, future research must also focus on teacher learning about and use of differentiated instruction because what we do know from previous empirical evidence is that many physical education teachers say that they lack the knowledge, skills, experience and confidence to plan for and teach students with diverse learning needs (Morley et al., 2021). Here, there needs to be specific focus on learning about and utilising differentiated instruction in relation to content, process, product and learning environment given that these have been identified as its core principles and areas of focus (Colquitt et al., 2017; van Munster et al., 2019).

Reverse Integration

The school has recently received delivery of eight sports wheelchairs, donated by the local wheelchair basketball club. They're a little worn, even battered, but Michael doesn't care. He won't be using them anyway. He has his own. Mr Stanton, the physical education teacher, has been talking about the wheelchairs and wheelchair activities for a few weeks now, and today is the first day of a six-week unit dedicated entirely to wheelchair activities. Michael is excited. He plays wheelchair basketball for the local team and is one of the better players. He is excited to show Mr Stanton and the other students what he can do. The lesson starts with a safety briefing and some tips and activities to help the students to familiarise themselves with the wheelchairs. They start by learning the basics – start, stop, turn and rotate. Next, they very slowly progress to weaving in-between cones. Michael, please give us a demonstration, *says Mr Stanton. Before the sentence is finished, Michael is whizzing in-between the cones with great speed and precision. He even does a wheelie at the end and returns through the cones in reverse because, you know, he can.* Wow, that is cool, *says one student.* Show off, *adds another.*

Reverse integration in physical education, oftentimes referred to as disability sport, which involves nondisabled people participating in activities developed primarily for – sometimes by – disabled people are often used during teacher education programmes to better pre-pare pre-service teachers for teaching disabled students. Moreover, they are sometimes used by physical education teachers in physical education. While it is the teacher who decides what the aim and pur-pose of reverse integration is, and thus the pedagogical approach un-derpinning it, empirical research suggests that reverse integration can increase the confidence of disabled wheelchair users because it pro-vides an opportunity for them to showcase their abilities to teachers and age-peers (Spencer-Cavaliere & Watkinson 2010). In addition, the parents of disabled wheelchair users in research by Carter and col-leagues (2014) reported positive change in willingness and ability of their disabled child to mix in a group, make friends, develop social skills such as communication, and increased confidence because of participating in reverse integration activities. In a similar vein, Lyons and colleagues (2009) noted that parents reported that their disabled child gained enhanced self-confidence, social skills and a stronger be-lief in self because of reverse integration approaches.

There is research suggesting that reverse integration activities impact positively on nondisabled students too. Much of the research in this field is tied to using reverse integration to increase awareness of disa-bility and stimulate attitudinal change towards disabled people and is, thus, either directly or directly based on some form of contact theory (Allport, 1954). According to Allport (1935), as people encounter others perceived to be different from themselves, their prejudiced beliefs abate as they come to accept and understand the other person. In this respect, McKay and colleagues (2021) argue that reverse integration approaches, or disability awareness activities as they call them, should be focused on four specific areas to stimulate the required attitudinal change: (a) equal status, (b) pursing common cooperative goals, (c) intimate (meaningful) interactions and (d) community/authority support. While not explicitly underpinned by contact theory, research by Evans and colleagues (2015) suggests that nondisabled students developed more positive beliefs about the bodies and abilities of disabled wheelchair users, especially in relation to the physical demands associated with using a wheelchair, after participating in a 12-week wheelchair basketball programme. This research and its finding aligned with and was extended by the parents of nondisabled children in research by Carter and colleagues (2014), who suggested that reverse integration supported their children to *learn that everyone is equal, think about disabled children more, gain an understand-ing of the difficulties of a wheelchair user, understand how hard it is to move in a wheelchair* and *develop new skills.*

In sum, there is reasonable research and practitioner evidence supporting the claim that reverse integration activities can impact positively on the self-confidence and wider perceptions of self among wheelchair users in physical education. What we do not know yet is the ways and extent to which this increased confidence transfers to different contexts and situations. Similarly, there is convincing evidence suggesting that reverse integration activities can impact positively on the attitudes of nondisabled students towards disabled students, but little is known about the longevity or contextual nature of such attitude change. Is this attitudinal change ephemeral and context-dependent, or is it deeply embedded and long-lasting? This is for future researchers to explore. Long-term, sustainable attitudinal change is important given that most of the time spent in physical education focusing on activities developed by nondisabled people for nondisabled people.

Conclusion

This chapter provides a brief overview of physical disability, before exploring, using creative nonfiction accounts and discussions of published literature, strategies that are most frequently promoted and used when teaching physical education to physically disabled students. While we hope that this chapter has given you some ideas to consider relating to planning for *inclusion* through the use of universal design for learning, using differentiated instruction to personalise pedagogical actions, and reverse integration as an alternative to traditional approaches and activities that were designed for nondisabled people, we also encourage you to be critical of the research-based supporting these practitioners. Indeed, the onus here is on teachers to engage in pedagogical experimentation to see what works best for whom in what settings and under what conditions because, from an academic perspective, the research supporting them is still in its infancy and needs developing.

References

Allport, G. W. (1935). Attitudes. In C. Murchison (Ed.), *A handbook of social psychology* (pp. 798–844). Clark University Press.

Allport, G. W. (1954). *The nature of prejudice.* Addison-Wesley.

Block, M. (Ed.). (2016). *A teacher's guide to adapted physical education: Including students with disabilities in sports and recreation* (4th ed.). Paul H. Brookes.

Block, M., Haegele, J., Kelly, L., & Obrusnikova, I. (2021). Exploring future research in adapted physical education. *Research Quarterly for Exercise and Sport, 92*(3), 429–442. https://doi.org/10.1080/02701367.2020.1741500

Brian, A., Grenier, M., Lieberman, L. J., Egan, C., & Taunton, S. (2017). 50 million strong for all: Universally designing CSPAPs to align with APE best practices. *Journal of Physical Education, Recreation & Dance, 88*(7), 30–36. http://doi.org/10.1080/07303084.2017.1340206

Carter, B., Grey, J., McWilliams, E., Clair, Z., Blake, K., & Byatt, R. (2014) 'Just kids playing sport (in a chair)': Experiences of children, families and stakeholders attending a wheelchair sports club. *Disability & Society, 29*(6), 938–952. https://doi.org/10.1080/09687599.2014.880329

CAST. (2018). Universal design for learning guidelines version 2.2. http://udlguidelines.cast.org

Centre for Disease Control and Prevention (CDC). (2022). Disability impacts all of us. https://www.cdc.gov/ncbddd/disabilityandhealth/infographic-disability- impacts-all.html

Colquitt, G., Pritchard, T., Johnson, C., & McCollum, S. (2017). Differentiating instruction in physical education: Personalization of learning. *Journal of Physical Education, Recreation & Dance, 88*(7), 44–50. https://doi.org/10.1080/07303084.2017.1340205

Department for Work and Pensions. (2021). *Family resources survey: Financial year 2019–2020.* Department for Work and Pensions.

Evans, A., Bright, J., & Brown, L. (2015). Non-disabled secondary school children's lived experiences of a wheelchair basketball programme delivered in the east of England. *Sport, Education and Society*, 20(6), 741–761. https://doi.org/10.1080/13573322.2013.808620

Gilbert, E. (2019). Designing inclusive physical education with universal design for learning. *Journal of Physical Education, Recreation & Dance, 90*(7), 15–21. https://doi.org/10.1080/07303084.2019.1637305

Government Equalities Office. (2010). *The Equality Act 2010.* https://www.legislation.gov.uk/ukpga/2010/15/contents

Grenier, M., Miller, N., & Black, K. (2017). Applying universal design for learning and the inclusion spectrum for students with severe disabilities in general physical education. *Journal of Physical Education, Recreation & Dance, 88*(6), 51–56. https://doi.org/10.1080/07303084.2017.1330167

Haegele, J. A., & Maher, A. J. (2022). Male autistic youth experiences of inclusion and feelings of belonging in integrated physical education. *Autism, 26*(1), 51–61. https://doi.org/10.1177%2F13623613211018637

Hutzler, Y. (2020) Evidence-based practices in adapted physical education. In J. Haegele, S. Hodge, & D. Shapiro (Eds.), *Routledge handbook of adapted physical education* (pp. 95–113). Routledge.

Jarvis, J., Pill, S., & Noble, A. (2017). Differentiated pedagogy to address learner diversity in secondary physical education. *Journal of Physical Education, Recreation & Dance, 88*(8), 46–54. https://doi.org/10.1080/07303084.2017.1356771

Kennedy, W., & Yun, J. (2019). Universal design for learning as a curriculum development tool in physical education. *Journal of Physical Education, Recreation & Dance, 90*(6), 25–31. https://doi.org/10.1080/07303084.2019.1614119

King-Sears, M. (2020). Introduction to special series on universal design for learning. *Remedial and Special Education, 41*(4), 191–193. https://doi.org/10.1177%2F0741932520908342

Lieberman, L., & Grenier, M. (2019). Infusing universal design for learning into physical education professional preparation programs. *Journal of Physical Education, Recreation & Dance, 90*(6), 3–5. https://doi.org/10.1080/07303084.2019.1615790

Lieberman, L., Grenier, M., Brian, A., & Arndt, K. (Eds.). (2020). *Universal design for learning in physical education*. Human Kinetics.

Lieberman, L. J., & Houston-Wilson, C. (2018). *Strategies for inclusion: Physical education for all* (3rd ed.). Human Kinetics.

Lieberman, L. J., Lytle, R. K., & Clarcq, J. A. (2008). Getting it right from the start: Employing the universal design for learning approach to your curriculum. *Journal of Physical Education, Recreation & Dance, 79*(2), 32–39. https://doi.org/10.1080/07303084.2008.10598132

Lyons, S., Corneille, D., Coker, P., & Ellis, C. (2009). A miracle in the outfield: The benefits of participation in organized baseball leagues for children with mental and physical disabilities. *Therapeutic Recreation Journal, 43*(3), 41–48.

Maher, A. J., & Fitzgerald, H. (2020). The culture of special schools: The nature, purpose and value of physical education. *Educational Review* [online first]. https://doi.org/10.1080/00131911.2020.1721437

Maher, A. J., Haegele, J., & Sparkes, A. (2021) "It's better than going into it blind": Reflections by people with visual impairments regarding the use of simulation for pedagogical purposes. *Sport, Education and Society* [online first]. https://doi.org/10.1080/13573322.2021.1897562

McKay, C., Haegele, J., & Pérez-Torralba, A. (2021). My perspective has changed on an entire group of people': Undergraduate students' experiences with the Paralympic Skill Lab. *Sport, Education and Society.* https://doi.org/10.1080/13573322.2021.1949702

Metzler, M., & Colquitt, G. (2021). *Instructional models for physical education.* Routledge.

Morley, D., Banks, T., Haslingden, C., Kirk, B., Parkinson, S., van Rossum, T., Morley, I. D., and Maher, A. J. (2021) Physical education teachers' views of including pupils with special educational needs and/or disabilities: A revisit study, *European Physical Education Review, 27*(2), 401–418. https://doi.org/10.1177/1356336X20953872

Ok, M.-W., Rao, K., Bryant, B., & McDougall, D. (2017). Universal design for learning in pre-k to grade 12 classrooms: A systematic review of research. *Exceptionality, 25*(2), 116–138. https://doi.org/10.1080/09362835.2016.1196450

Oliver, M. (2013). The social model of disability: Thirty years on. *Disability & Society, 28*(7), 1024–1026. https://doi.org/10.1080/09687599.2013.818773

Porretta, D. (2011). Cerebral brain injury, traumatic brain injury and stroke. In J. Winnick (Ed.), *Adapted physical education and sport* (pp. 269–290). Human Kinetics.

Santangelo, T., & Tomlinson, C. A. (2012). Teacher educators' perceptions and use of differentiated instruction practices: An exploratory investigation. *Action in Teacher Education, 34*, 309–327. https://doi.org/10.1080/01626620.2012.717032

Shields, N., Synnot, A., & Barr, M. (2012). Perceived barriers and facilitators to physical activity for children with disability: A systematic review. *British Journal of Sports Medicine, 46*(14), 989–997. http://doi.org/10.1136/bjsports-2011-090236

Spencer-Cavaliere, N., & Watkinson, E. (2010). Inclusion understood from the perspectives of children with disability. *Adapted Physical Activity Quarterly, 27*(4), 275–293. https://doi.org/10.1123/apaq.27.4.275

Tomlinson, C. A. (1995). Deciding to differentiate instruction in middle school: One school's journey. *Gifted Child Quarterly, 39*, 77–87. https://doi.org/10.1177%2F001698629503900204

Tomlinson, C. A. (2014). *The differentiated classroom: Responding to the needs of all learners* (2nd ed.). Association for Supervision and Curriculum Development.

Tomlinson, C. A., & Imbeau, M. B. (2010). *Leading and managing a differentiated classroom.* Association for Supervision and Curriculum Development.

US Census Bureau. (2019). *Childhood disability in the United States: 2019.* US Department of Commerce. https://www.census.gov/content/dam/Census/library/publications/2021/acs/acsbr-006.pdf

Van Munster, Lieberman, L., & Grenier, M. (2019) Universal design for learning and differentiated instruction in physical education. *Adapted Physical Activity Quarterly, 19*(36), 359–377 https://doi.org/10.1123/apaq.2018-0145

Winnick, J. P., & Porretta, D. L. (2017). *Adapted physical education and sports* (6th ed.). Human Kinetics.

7 Teaching Blind or Visually Impaired Students in Physical Education

Background and Context

Visual impairment is an umbrella term often used to refer to a range of visual function from low vision through total blindness that is not correctable using even the strongest prescription eyeglasses and interferes with tasks of daily life. According to the World Health Organization (WHO, 2014), about 285 million people are estimated to have low vision (246 million people) and legal blindness (39 million people) worldwide. Importantly, a large proportion of visually impaired people are elderly, as visual impairment is closely associated with aging. As such, it is unsurprising that about 65% of the world's visually impaired population is 50 years old or older (WHO, 2014). The WHO (2014) estimates a range of 0.2 per thousand to 1.2 per thousand children are blind in high-income and low-income regions, respectively. In addition, the WHO (2014) estimates that the rate of low vision is approximately 3x that of blindness among children. In the United Kingdom, there are over 2 million visually impaired people, including over 25,000 children aged 16 years or under (Royal National Institute of Blind People, 2019). For our purposes, it is noteworthy that visually impaired children and young people tend to exhibit poorer postural control (Pennell, 2021) and perceived and actual motor competence (Brian et al., 2019, 2020). Additionally, visually impaired adults reflecting about their experiences in physical education have commonly reported unfavourable experiences, oftentimes characterised by instances of marginalisation, exclusion and bullying (Haegele & Kirk, 2018; Haegele et al., 2020; Haegele & Zhu, 2017). These unfavourable experiences can track into adulthood, and influence visually impaired adults to divert away from physical activity for more sedentary pursuits (Yessick & Haegele, 2018).

DOI: 10.4324/9781003176282-7

Overview of Visual Impairment

Generally, bio-medical definitions centred on visual acuity, visual field or aetiology of visual impairment are dominant in scholarship, practice and policy (Lieberman & Ball, 2022; WHO, 2014). Visual acuity refers to the clarity of vision (Lieberman & Ball, 2022). A 20/20 visual acuity is often referred to as *average vision* and means that a person can read a standard eye chart at a distance of 20 feet away. In contrast, 20/200 visual acuity means that a person can see at 20 feet with the clarity of what a person with 20/20 vision can see at 200 feet. Visual field refers to the area that can be seen when the eye is focused on a certain point (Lieberman & Ball, 2022). An average visual field is about 120 degrees horizontally. Under the umbrella term of visual impairment, the acuity or field of vision can be organised using terms like *low vision*, *legal blindness* or *total blindness*, each of which referring to a different degree of impairment. For example, low vision, a term often used in the United States to describe the least impactful degree of visual impairment, is typically associated with a visual acuity that is 20/70 or worse (Lieberman & Ball, 2022; Lieberman et al., 2013). Legal blindness, which generally refers to individuals with some usable vision, refers to individuals who have either a visual acuity of 20/200 or less or a visual field of 20 degrees or less in their better eye with the best possible correction (WHO, 2014). Many legally blind people have some usable vision, and few read braille or use mobility devices like long white canes or guide dogs. Finally, individual who have no light perception in either eye, which generally is inclusive of most individuals who read braille and use mobility devices, may be considered having total blindness.

Visual impairment is also regularly discussed in terms of aetiology. There are many causes of visual impairment, some that are congenital (before birth) or adventitious (acquired later in life), as well as progressive (more impactful over time) and stable (does not change). As recent as ten years ago, the most common bio-medical causes of visual impairment among children and young people internationally were congenital cataracts, albinism, retinopathy of prematurity, optic atrophy and optic nerve hypoplasia (WHO, 2014). However, recent years has seen cortical (or cerebral) visual impairment (CVI) become the most common cause of visual impairment in children and young people in developed countries, including the United Kingdom (Royal National Institute of Blind People, 2019). According to Pehere and colleagues (2018), this is likely due to medical advancements in the management of treatable causes of childhood blindness (such as cataract, glaucoma and retinopathy of prematurity) as well as increased reporting of CVI.

Aim and Purpose

The aim of this chapter is to explore and critique strategies that are discussed and promoted in academic literature to teach visually impaired students in physical education. To do this, brief creative non-fiction stories are provided relating to the experiences of a visually impaired student, Toby, and a blind student, Wanda, as well as various stakeholders that they interact with in their classes. The strategies used in these accounts, selected because they are commonly depicted in practice-based materials suggesting pedagogical practices for teachings visually impaired students, are then discussed and critiqued utilising the existing research base. Particular focus is placed on leveraging research seeking to amplify the voices of visually impaired people. This aligns with our goal to encourage schools to engage in research-based practices that are vetted by visually impaired persons when engaging in their education.

Learning Support Assistants

As Wanda enters the sports hall, grinning widely at the thought of a new physical education unit beginning today, Ms Susan, learning support assistant, walks in a half step behind her. Ms Susan started working with Wanda during physical education a few years ago, when Wanda was accidently struck by a ball during class, and safety concerns were voiced by her parents. Physical education classes always begin with running circles in Mr Smith's class, but not for Wanda, who is walking the inside of the circle with Ms Susan. When Mr Smith begins to take role and announce upcoming activities to the class, Ms Susan is close by Wanda explaining various physical cues that Mr Smith provides. Activities then commence, and students are kicking balls in small groups to practice their kicking and trapping form. Wanda is now off to the side of the sports hall with Ms Susan, practicing the same activity but just the two of them. At Wanda's request, Ms Susan asks Mr Smith if Wanda should be participating with the other kids, but within the conversation they agree that it is a safer bet to keep Wanda separated from the others.

The terms learning support assistant, paraeducators or teacher aids generally refer to an adult who works with and alongside educators in classrooms and other educational settings to support the educational needs of students (Lieberman & Conroy, 2013). The use of one-to-one learning support assistants, in particular, has become one of the primary mechanisms by which disabled students, including visually impaired students, receive instructional, social and physical needs support throughout the school day, including in physical education (Haegele et al., 2019). Supporting this, the utilisation of paraeducators or teacher aids has been recommended extensively when working with disabled students in physical education (Lieberman, 2007), including an extensive collection of books (Lieberman et al., 2013), book chapters (Haegele & Lieberman, 2019; Lieberman & Ball, 2022) and practitioner-based papers (Lieberman et al., 2019) that discuss visually impaired students specifically. According to Lieberman and colleagues (2013), paraeducators can work

> alongside the physical education teacher to ensure that the students with visual impairment or deafblindness are receiving the intended benefits from physical education class, regardless of whether physical education is provided in an inclusive setting with nondisabled students, in a modified setting, or in a separate class.
> (p. 49)

Generally, this role is expected to include paraeducators assisting students through movements, keeping students focused on tasks, providing supplemental verbal and physical prompts and repeating instructions if needed (Lieberman, 2007; Lieberman & Conroy, 2013). Importantly, each of the resources that explicate the benefits of learning support assistants in physical education explain the need for them to be trained in physical education settings, so that they have the requisite knowledge to provide context specific instruction and assistance (e.g., Lieberman et al., 2013; Lieberman & Ball, 2022).

Unfortunately, research exploring the utilisation of learning support assistants in physical education classes for visually impaired students demonstrates that training in these contexts and for these professionals is rare (Lieberman & Conroy, 2013), and therefore they may not be equipped with the knowledge, skill or experience to effectively contribute to students' physical education experiences (Maher, 2016). Given this lack of training, it is perhaps unsurprising that visually impaired individuals have reflected negatively about their experiences with learning support assistants when describing their experiences in physical education (Haegele et al., 2019). For example, in a study discussing experiences of visually impaired adults, participants described instances where the lack of training of learning support assistants was obvious, and they were clearly disengaged or disinterested throughout the class (Haegele et al., 2019). Conflictingly, though, overly involved learning support assistants, who *helped* participants at the demise of social interactions and friendship development, have also been recalled. These learning support assistants, perhaps like Ms Susan, can exacerbate social issues between students by providing unwanted or unneeded assistance that can influence unwanted social attention and isolation from peers (Haegele et al., 2019). This may speak to the undefined and ambiguous roles and responsibilities of learning support assistants in physical education (Bryan et al., 2013; Maher, 2016) who often appear to exist on opposing poles of a continuum of help, either overhelping visually impaired students or sitting at the side disengaged. This line of inquiry shouldn't deter the use of learning support assistants in physical education, but rather should highlight the necessity for thoughtful and appropriate training. This training should include strategies to openly and actively communicate with visually impaired students about their wants and needs, so that learning support assistants are working within the best interest of each individual student.

One-to-one Peer Tutoring

Mr Smith sees Toby struggling in physical education activities, and wonders what he might be able to do to provide more support. Thinking Toby might benefit from having another person to work closely with, Mr Smith recalls that Toby is close with one of his classmates, Harry. Mr Smith approaches Harry after class, asking 'Hey, Harry, would you be interested in helping Toby out during P.E. some days? If so, maybe you can join me before our next class and we can talk about it a bit with him?'. *In agreement, Harry and Mr Smith, and now Toby as well, meet to discuss peer tutoring roles and responsibilities, to which each party agrees. When class begins, it seems like a quick success, where Harry is working with Toby to help explain various tasks, and provide help and advice where needed.*

Peer tutoring has been described as an innovative pedagogical tool in physical education (Cervantes et al., 2013), which can take on several forms, including one-to-one peer tutoring, class wide peer tutoring and reciprocal peer tutoring. One to-one peer-tutoring, the most likely selected form in most physical education contexts, generally occurs with established pairs where a nondisabled student is trained and positioned as the tutor, and a disabled student of roughly the same age will be positioned as the peer. A perceived benefit of this form of peer tutoring, according to Cervantes and colleagues (2013), is that 'both students know their role' (p. 44). One-to-one peer tutoring has become a popular recommendation in practice-based texts because of assumed social and health benefits, enhanced learning and participation and feelings of inclusion (Kalef et al., 2013). As such, there are numerous documents that provide instructions on how to set-up and implement one-to-one peer tutoring models within the classroom when integrating disabled students, including visually impaired students (Cervantes et al., 2013; Houston-Wilson et al., 1997).

Unlike many pedagogical practices adopted in physical education and recommended in practitioner-oriented works, there is some empirical evidence to support the utility of this practice, particularly regarding supporting motor skill learning (Wiskochil et al., 2007). In their study, Wiskochil and colleagues (2007) noted improvements in academic learning time in physical education among visually impaired students when engaged in a one-to-one peer tutoring model. However, it is noteworthy that, as voiced by Kalef and colleagues (2013), considering trained peer tutors as an evidence-based practice may be premature, given the quality and depth of available research in this area. That is, despite peer tutoring having a reputation as a practice with a substantial research base, few studies exist that support its utility. Concerns of a lack of research supporting this, and other, pedagogical practices are allayed by the dearth of work discussing this practice with visually impaired persons themselves. As such, we do not intend to suggest discarding one-to-one peer tutoring as a potential meaningful pedagogical practice, however recognise that dialogue with visually impaired pupils about its conceptualisation and delivery is critical to understanding its value.

Tactile Modelling and Physical Guidance

Mr Smith is in the early days of his elementary school unit, teaching various movement concepts like hopping, skipping and jumping. Typically, this instruction includes a heavy reliance on visual models, where he performs the task in front of his class before asking his students to emulate his movement. He's noticed, though, that Wanda is not performing the skills according to his instruction. When he approaches Wanda, she says that 'sometimes in Ms Green's music class, when I need help understanding something physical, she will let me touch her hand or arm as she does the movement or activity, can we try that?'. *Mr Smith agrees, and after a few attempts, Wanda's form has improved. Mr Smith then explained that* 'your form is better, but there is a small change that's hard to explain. Can I move your arm and show you?'. *After Wanda consents, Mr Smith moves her arm slightly to perfect her form for the movement.*

Tactile modelling and physical guidance are modelling techniques often encouraged and implemented when teaching blind students, like Wanda (Lieberman et al., 2013, 2019; O'Connell et al., 2006). Modelling techniques are used to help individuals develop a mental picture of how a skill or activity is performed, which should help them to reproduce the skill. Tactile modelling, also known as hand-under-hand instruction, is a technique whereby blind students explore a movement by touching a model's (typically the instructor's) body while they demonstrate the movement (O'Connell et al., 2006). Those who advocate for the use of this modelling strategy suggest that tactile modelling can help clarify misunderstandings of movements more comprehensively than other pedagogical strategies, such as verbal instruction, and can allow students to move at their own learning pace (Lieberman et al., 2019). Physical guidance, or hand-over-hand instruction, is a second modelling technique often suggested which is reciprocal to tactile modelling, whereby the pupil's body is being physically moved (or, guided) by the instructor (Lieberman et al., 2013). According to O'Connell and colleagues (2006) physical guidance is typically used to help individuals to understand the rhythm and motion of a movement.

Despite the proliferation of practice-oriented documents suggesting tactile modelling and physical guidance in physical education contexts when teaching blind students (Lieberman & Linsenbigler, 2017; Lieberman et al., 2019; O'Connell et al., 2006), empirical support for these strategies is lacking. As such, it appears that their recommendation represents a best practice which is based on anecdotal information or personal experiences of instructors or authors, rather than research informed practice. As such, tactile modelling and physical guidance exemplify the (dis)connection between research and practice that drives the central focus of this book. This is not to say that no research in physical education spaces has utility in contributing to our understanding of the use of modelling techniques for blind students. For example, blind and visually impaired adults have reflected about the utility of touch as a pedagogical tool in physical education contexts, which is central to both of the aforementioned modelling techniques (Maher et al., 2021). However, studies focused directly on the utility of these modelling techniques is absent from the literature. Notably, the importance of consent and consistent conversations in relation to touching the body of others (Maher et al., 2021; Yessick & Haegele, 2018), to allow students to dictate the magnitude and frequency of the utilisation of this pedagogical tool, has been suggested. This can help teachers avoid what Bourdieu (1991) refers to as *symbolic violence*, in instances where teachers initiate touch when it is not expected or consented to.

Boundary, Equipment and Rule Modifications

Mr Smith is an avid basketball player, spending hours at a local park on weekends playing with neighbours and friends. As such, basketball is clearly his favourite activity to teach, and he wants everyone to partici-pate. Toby is apprehensive in basketball games but is keen to share with a classmate a strategy he's developed 'I just run up and down the court with the crowd, and try not to get in anyone's way'. For Toby, this works. His vision means that if a ball is thrown to him, he likely won't react quickly enough to accurately judge it, and he's unlikely to catch it or throw it accurately to a teammate. Just as the game is underway, Mr Smith has some surprises for Toby and his classmates. 'Today, we're going to use a brightly coloured yellow basketball, and I have a new rule, everyone must touch the ball before shooting'. *Toby's stomach sinks, knowing his cover has been blown. While playing, he feels exposed. This feeling peaks when a classmate yells* 'come on Toby, touch the ball so we can keep playing', *to which he walked off the court and sat down.*

Activity modifications, which can include boundary, equipment and rule modifications, are changes that a teacher makes to the space of the activity, environment, equipment or rules or speed of a game or activity within a lesson (Lieberman et al., 2019). As per recommen-dations by Lieberman and colleagues (2019), 'some key activity and fitness modifications may include the use of auditory equipment, the provision of tactile boundaries, the use of aerobic fitness equipment that is stationary, and the inclusion of guides or tethers for running activities' (p. 35). These modifications can range from using larger or brightly coloured balls, including sound sources or bells within equip-ment, allowing more bounces or asking everyone to touch a ball before shooting on a goal or putting sound sources behind goals. Modifica-tions like this are oft presented in practice-oriented materials with the intention of providing ideas of ways to adapt physical education classes and teaching to effectively educate visually impaired students (Haegele & Lieberman, 2019; Lieberman et al., 2019). Importantly, the need for modifications is likely different depending on the student and their unique needs, and therefore physical educators are encouraged to speak with the student, as well as other knowledgeable stakehold-ers, prior to selecting and implementing modifications (Haegele & Lieberman, 2019).

While boundary, equipment and rule modifications may appear to be rooted in logical thought, the proliferation of these in practice-based materials may be of some concern from an empirical standpoint. That is, there is little, if any, empirical support for these strategies. Rather, it appears possible that these *common-sense* recommendations benefit teachers and other stakeholders, who adopt them because of the trust they place in the social capital of those recommending them and the desire for them to feel as though they are *including* disabled students. Regardless of this positive intention, it is possible that such strategies may do more harm than good by highlighting the incapability of the body, reproducing able-bodiedness and invalidating the abilities of disabled youth in physical education (Haegele & Zhu, 2017; Haegele et al., 2020). While perhaps there are some benefits of these modifications, at the very least we strongly encourage that (a) pseudo-experts who recommend these modifications consult with visually impaired persons prior to their dissemination and soften language about claims regarding the benefits of their implementation; and (b) teachers and other instructional personnel discuss modifications with students before implementing these strategies to ensure they are aligned with their needs and wants.

Conclusion

This chapter provides a brief overview of visual impairment and visually impaired children and young people, before exploring, using vignettes and a discussion of published literature, strategies that are most frequently promoted and used when teaching visually impaired students in physical education. This chapter provides narratives discussing the use of learning support assistants; peer tutors; tactile modelling and physical guidance and boundary, equipment and rule modifications. It is perhaps not surprising that visually impaired people tend to report challenging experiences within physical education (e.g., Haegele et al., 2020) given that many pedagogical practices that are adopted are based more so on *expert* advice rather than empirical data or visually impaired persons' experiences and perspectives. For us, it is critical to continue to recommend that physical educators consider these pedagogical practices only when also engaging with visually impaired students about their wants and needs.

References

Bourdieu, P. (1991). *Language and symbolic power.* Harvard University Press.

Brian, A., De Meester, A., Klavina, A., Irwin, J. M., Taunton, S., Pennell, A., & Lieberman, L. J. (2019). Exploring children with visual impairments' physical literacy: A preliminary investigation of autonomous motivation. *Journal of Teaching in Physical Education, 38*(2), 155–161. https://doi.org/10.1123/jtpe.2018-0194

Brian, A., Starrett, A., Beach, P., De Meester, A., Pennell, A., Taunton Miedema, S., & Lieberman, L. J. (2020). Perceived motor competence mediates gross motor skills predicting physical activity in youth with visual impairments. *Research Quarterly for Exercise and Sport.* Epub available ahead of print. https://doi.org/10.1080/02701367.2020.1831688

Bryan, R. R., McCubbin, J., & van der Mars, H. (2013). The ambiguous role of the paraeducator in the general physical education environment. *Adapted Physical Activity Quarterly, 30*(2), 164–183. https://doi.org/10.1123/apaq.30.2.164

Cervantes, C., Lieberman, L. J., Magnesio, B., & Wood, J. (2013). Peer tutoring: Meeting the demands of inclusion in physical education today. *Journal of Physical Education, Recreation, & Dance, 84*(3), 43–48. https://doi.org/10.1080/07303084.2013.767712

Haegele, J. A., Hodge, S. R., Zhu, X., Holland, S. K., & Wilson, W. J. (2020). Understanding the inclusiveness of integrated physical education from the perspectives of adults with visual impairments. *Adapted Physical Activity Quarterly, 37*(2), 141–159. https://doi.org/10.1123/apaq.2019-0094

Haegele, J. A., & Kirk, T. N. (2018). Experiences in physical education: Exploring the intersection of visual impairment and maleness. *Adapted Physical Activity Quarterly, 35*(2), 196–213. https://doi.org/10.1123/apaq.2017-0132

Haegele, J. A., & Lieberman, L. J. (2019). Movement and visual impairment. In J. Ravenscroft (Ed.), *The Routledge handbook of visual impairment* (pp. 189–202). Routledge.

Haegele, J. A., Sato, T., Zhu, X., & Kirk, T. N. (2019). Paraeducator support in integrated physical education as reflected by adults with visual impairments. *Adapted Physical Activity Quarterly, 36,* 91–108. https://doi.org/10.1123/apaq.2018-0063

Haegele, J. A., & Zhu, X. (2017). Experiences of individuals with visual impairments in integrated physical education: A retrospective study. *Research Quarterly for Exercise & Sport, 88*(4), 425–435. https://doi.org/10.1080/02701367.2017.1346781

Houston-Wilson, C., Lieberman, L., Horton, M., & Kasser, S. (1997). Peer tutoring: A plan for instructing students of all abilities. *Journal of Physical Education, Recreation & Dance, 68*(6), 39–44. https://doi.org/10.1080/07303084.1997.10604964

Kalef, L., Reid, G., & MacDonald, C. (2013). Evidence-based practice: A quality indicator analysis of peer-tutoring in adapted physical education. *Research in Developmental Disabilities, 24,* 2514–2522. https://doi.org/10.1016/j.ridd.2013.05.004

Lieberman, L. J. (2007). *Paraeducators in physical education: A training guide to role and responsibilities.* Human Kinetics.

Lieberman, L. J., & Ball, L. (2022). Visual impairments. In J. P. Winnick & D. L Porretta (Eds.), *Adapted physical education and sport* (7th ed., pp. 233–249). Human Kinetics.

Lieberman, L. J., & Conroy, P. (2013). Training of paraeducators for physical education for children with visual impairments. *Journal of Visual Impairment & Blindness, 107*(1), 17–28. https://doi.org/10.1177%2F0145482X1310700102

Lieberman, L. J., Lepore, M., Lepore-Stevens, M., & Ball, L. (2019). Physical education for children with visual impairment or blindness. *Journal of Physical Education, Recreation, & Dance, 90*(1), 30–38. http://doi.org/10.1080/07303084.2018.1535340

Lieberman, L. J., & Linsenbigler, K. (2017). Teaching recreational activities to children and youth with visual impairment or deafblindness. *Palaestra, 31*(1), 40–46.

Lieberman, L. J., Ponchillia, P. E., & Ponchillia, S. V. (2013). *Physical education and sport for people with visual impairments and deafblindness: Foundations for instruction.* AFB Press.

Maher, A. J. (2016). Special educational needs in mainstream secondary school physical education: Learning support assistants have their say. *Sport, Education and Society, 21*(2), 262–278. https://doi.org/10.1080/13573322.2014.905464

Maher, A. J., Haegele, J. A., & Sparkes, A. C. (2021). 'It's better than going into it blind': Reflections by people with visual impairments regarding the use of simulations for pedagogical purposes. *Sport, Education & Society.* Available online ahead of print at https://doi.org/10.1080/13573322.2021.1897562

O'Connell, M., Lieberman, L. J., & Petersen, S. (2006). The use of tactile modelling and physical guidance as instructional strategies in physical activity for children who are blind, *Journal of Visual Impairment & Blindness, 100*(8), 471–477.

Pehere, N., Chougule, P., & Dutton, G. N. (2018). Cerebral visual impairment in children: Causes and associated ophthalmological problems. *Indian Journal of Ophthalmology, 66*(6), 812–815. https://doi.org/10.4103%2Fijo.IJO_1274_17

Pennell, A. (2021). Postural control and balance. In J. A. Haegele (Ed.), *Movement & visual impairment: Research across disciplines* (pp. 17–31). Routledge.

Royal National Institute of Blind People. (2019). *Key information and statistics on sight loss in the UK.* Author. https://www.rnib.org.uk/professionals/knowledge-and- research-hub/key-information-and-statistics.

Wiskochil, B., Lieberman, L., Houston-Wilson, C., & Petersen, S. (2007). The effects of trained peer tutors on academic learning time–physical education on four children who are visually impaired or blind. *Journal of Visual Impairment and Blindness, 101*, 339–350.

World Health Organization. (2014). *Visual impairment and blindness.* Author. https://web.archive.org/web/20150512062236/http://www.who.int/mediacentre/factsheets/fs282/en/

Yessick, A. B., & Haegele, J. A. (2018). "Missed opportunities": Adults with visual impairments reflections on the impact of physical education on current physical activity. *British Journal of Visual Impairment, 37*(1), 40–49. https://doi.org/10.1177/0264619618814070

8 Conclusion and Recommendations
Understanding the (Dis)Connections

The aim of this book was to centre the role that evidence generally, and research specifically, can and does play in the development of pedagogical practices relating to teaching disabled students in physical education. Specifically, we aimed to examine, interrogate and problematise the evidence and research base of several practices that are used and even advocated for by teachers and researchers when it comes to teaching autistic students, Deaf students, students experiencing cognitive or learning disability, physically disabled students and visually impaired students. In the first chapter, entitled *Foundational Information for Teaching Disabled Children in Physical Education*, we explored the models of disability to argue that the ways in which teachers conceptualise disability, and thus the emphasis they place on its bio-medical and/or social-cultural aspects, is crucial because that will shape the curriculums they develop, their pedagogical actions and the assessments they use to judge the learning and development of disabled students (Vickerman & Maher, 2018). To add, teachers' ideologies and beliefs about disability will also influence the learning environments that they construct, their interactions and relationship with disabled students, and the ways and extent to which disabled students feel that they belong, are accepted and are valued in the educational spaces they find themselves (Haegele & Maher, 2021, 2022).

The same, it must be said, goes for how teachers conceptualise inclusion. Indeed, if you accept, as we do, that our ideologies and values shape our behaviours (Elias, 1978) – if given the expressive freedom to do so – then it follows that what you consider inclusion to be will influence how you endeavour to be inclusive. Therefore, if inclusion for you is about all students having access to the same setting and activities, that is how you as a teacher will plan for and teach physical education. To us, we must admit, this conceptualisation of inclusion

DOI: 10.4324/9781003176282–8

appears reductive and problematic, largely because it places focus on ensuring disabled and non-disabled students exist in the same physical space (Haegele & Maher, 2021) and ignores the meaning and satisfactions that students can and should derive from physical education (Martin Ginis et al., 2017) as well as negative experiences that have been depicted throughout research from the viewpoint of disabled students in the past decade or so (e.g., Alves et al., 2018; Haegele & Maher, 2021). Similarly, if you consider inclusion to be aligned with ideas about equity and equitable practices (Hodge et al., 2012), then you may focus more on making modifications and adaptations to the activities that are typically taught in physical education. However, if you adopt a student-centred approach to inclusion, as we do in this text, you will also be concerned about how disabled students – and, indeed, all students – feel before, during and after physical education.

As we have suggested elsewhere (see Haegele & Maher, 2021, 2022), the ways and extent to which disabled students feel a sense of belonging, acceptance and value in the spaces and groups they find themselves in during physical education should be key to how we judge the successes and failures of *inclusion*. This approach to inclusion extends beyond materiality and the physical existence of individuals within spaces and considers how people feel, cognitively and affectively, within that space interacting and connecting with others (Reich, 2010). If you agree with us here, and truly value the (physical education) experiences of disabled students, then please concern yourself with developing your knowledge and understanding about how your curriculum decisions, pedagogical practices and assessment arrangements, among many other things tied to the decisions that you make and what you do, shape how disabled students experience physical education. We have tried to help, albeit a little, in this respect by exploring the evidence and research base supporting (or not) some of the practices that are often used in physical education in the name of inclusion, paying particular attention to the presence (or absence) of research relating to what disabled students say about these practices.

What Does the Evidence Suggest?

There is strong empirical evidence supporting the claim that autistic students experience high rates of physical inactivity and obesity (Healy et al., 2017, 2019). Moreover, there is credible evidence, gathered mainly from autistic youth themselves, that they often experience marginalisation and bullying in integrated physical education especially (e.g., Haegele & Maher, 2021, 2022). When it comes to teaching autistic students, published literature focuses primarily but not exclusively on the use of structure and routines, applied behaviour analysis and its role within physical education and video modelling. Based on our critique, it appears that most strategies that are recommended for use in integrated physical education classes for autistic students have little empirical support in that specific setting. Rather, it appears that scholars are borrowing from research in other contexts and applying recommendations to this unique educational setting. Further, it appears that authors are supporting their recommendations by referencing prior non-empirical suggestions, creating a cycle of recommendations based on anecdotes and opinions. Of course, we are not suggesting that a structured learning environment and routinised practices are not of value and benefit; what we are saying is that there is hardly any research that explores, for instance, how the learning environment should be structured and routines developed and utilised, the influence of these practices on the learning and development of autistic youth, or even how they are experienced by autistic students in physical education. These are but a few of many areas of research that need the attention of our academic communities if we can recommend with confidence the practices often heralded as best practice for teaching autistic students in physical education.

When it comes to Deaf students, there is an abundance of empirical evidence suggesting that they are much more likely to have poorer balance (De Kegel et al., 2011; Majlesi et al., 2014), experiences delay in motor development (Rine et al., 2000) and be less physically active (Li et al., 2018; Lobenius-Palmér et al., 2018) than hearing students. Physical education can play an important role in narrowing but also exacerbating these disparities. Much of the published literature focuses on the position of the teacher during lessons, the use of non-verbal cues to communicate and for instructional purposes, using interpreters to facilitate communication and the use of peer-tutoring to support the learning and development of Deaf students. Given that some Deaf students need to see the faces and mouths of teachers to lip read, and teacher bodies when demonstrations are used, it seems obvious that teachers need to carefully consider where and how they position themselves. This is especially important for physical education teachers given that bodies are constantly moving during practical lessons and the learning environment can be frenetic. What is less obvious, because there is no research relating to it, is how teachers should position themselves throughout the lesson and use demonstrations to compliment verbal instructions when teaching Deaf students who lip read. Future research may want to consider using systematic observations to analyse teacher positioning. Technology may add a different and valuable dimension to research of this nature, such as using video analysis and thermal mapping to systematically track and/or use to support teachers and students to reflect on movement patterns. What is key here, from a research perspective, is that empirical data is gathered with, about and for Deaf students and their teachers and teaching assistants to develop a stronger knowledge and understanding of how best the latter can support the former in physical education. Even this is lacking from the extant literature relating to teaching Deaf students in physical education.

Students experiencing cognitive or learning difficulties, especially those with generalised movement difficulties, generally experience unfavourable circumstances in integrated physical education classes. This has been attributed to the low and negative expectations of their ability to perform in physical education by teachers and other students (Coates, 2011; Fitzgerald, 2005, 2012; Harvey et al., 2014). While there is a distinct lack of research relating to students who experience learning and cognitive difficulties in physical education, the literature that is available focuses on cooperative learning, micro-teaching tips and class organisation strategies. Although there is research evidence supporting some of these strategies among nondisabled students, with cooperative learning being a pedagogical model that has a strong and still growing research base, there is a notable lack of research supporting the use of these approaches for disabled students generally and those who experience cognitive or learning difficulties especially. This is despite several practice-based texts advocating for the use of them when teaching students who experience cognitive or learning difficulties (e.g., Grenier et al., 2005; Grenier & Yeaton, 2019; Mach, 2000). Without labouring a point that forms a key thread throughout this book, many of the practices advocated for teaching students experiencing cognitively or learning difficulties in physical education lack an empirical evidence base. We caution against assuming that what seems to work for nondisabled students in physical education will be appropriate for students who experience cognitive and learning difficulties. Thus, there is a need for theoretically guided and empirically informed research that explores, for instance, the influence of cooperative learning, micro-teaching tips and class organisation strategies on the learning and development – physical, cognitive, social and/or affective – of students who experience cognitive or learning difficulties.

Given the dominance of normative beliefs about the body, movement and performance, it is unsurprising that physically disabled students participate less frequently and in fewer activities than their nondisabled peers in physical education (e.g., Shields et al., 2012). Therefore, in this book we explored the research and wider evidence base relating to the utility of universal design for learning, differentiated instruction and reverse integration for teaching physically disabled students in physical education because those approaches are often advocated by academics and used by practitioners for teaching physically disabled students and their age-peers together (e.g., Carter et al., 2014; Lieberman & Houston-Wilson, 2018; Winnick & Poretta, 2017). While there is some published research literature supporting the use of reverse integration and differentiated instruction in physical education contexts, most of the literature relating to the utility of universal design for learning is published in practitioner texts and at present lacks a theoretically guided and empirically informed basis. This is not to say, of course, that universal design for learning does not or cannot impact positively on the learning and development of disabled students generally and physically disabled students specifically, like it seems to have done according to wider education research (see King-Sears, 2020; Ok et al., 2017). It does mean, however, that researchers need to explore the utility of universal design for learning in physical education because the subject's culture, learning environment, nature of social interactions and relationships, curriculums, pedagogies and assessment strategies are notably different from classroom subjects. Thus, we argue that researchers should not extrapolate those classroom-based findings to physical education.

Like many young disabled people, visually impaired pupils, including blind students, often reflect about having unfavourable experiences in physical education, oftentimes characterised by marginalisation and exclusion from activities (Haegele & Zhu, 2017, 2021). Hence, we critiqued strategies that are recommended for teaching and supporting visually impaired pupils in physical education, focusing specifically on the use of learning support assistants, peer tutoring, tactile modelling and physical guidance and activity modifications. In this respect, we argued that, while there is notable published literature suggesting the use of these strategies, little empirical data exists that supports their utility. Conflictingly, the value of most strategies presented have been critiqued, even criticised, by visually impaired individuals when reflecting on their experiences of physical education (Haegele et al., 2019, 2021).

So What?

What we know is that disabled students tend to report experiences within physical education classes that are unfavourable and negative

(Haegele & Maher, 2021; Holland & Haegele, 2020), and that teachers generally feel ill-equipped to instruct disabled students within their classes (Morley et al., 2021). What the construction of this text has taught us, as authors and scholars, is that the collective *we* (physical education researchers) are complicit in the construction and support of poor experiences of disabled students and insufficient training of teachers. That is, in reviewing and digesting published empirical work to gain clarity of (dis)connections between research and practice for this book, it has become clear that connections are not feasible, given the dearth of research that has explored pedagogical practices for teaching disabled students in physical education contexts. As such, we suggest that higher education academics who have been tasked with engaging in the knowledge-centred development and dissemination of pedagogical strategies for disabled students have fallen short of this goal and are contributing to the ill-equipped nature of educators to acknowledge and plan for disabled students within their classes (Flintoff & Fitzgerald, 2012; Penney et al., 2018).

What we have found is a mass proliferation of practice-based texts and journal articles that disseminate *best* practices without much consideration for the empirical support needed to guide their recommendations. Importantly, this includes studies that have amplified disabled person's voices about their experiences. Examples of this behaviour are exposed in each chapter of this text, where scholars are recommending practices for teachers to utilise within integrated physical education classes when teaching disabled students, without the accompaniment of much empirical data to confirm (or, deny) the appropriateness of those practices. It is challenging for us to postulate on reasons why this behaviour has gained traction in our field globally, and for teaching disabled students more specifically. It is, perhaps, possible that the publication of these artifacts is to support the needs of hubris-centric *expert* university staff, who feel a strong, and perhaps false, need to ensure disabled students are integrated into classes, and therefore disseminate largely unsupported practices that they *believe* work because of their *expertiseism*. This may be an unfair criticism of the practice, one that we have admittedly contributed to, however until academics and complicit practice-based resources adopt safeguards against this process, such as requiring practice-based content to be connected to empirical work, it is one that we must consider to be possible.

Perhaps scholars have positive intentions when writing and publishing such practice-based texts and articles, such as seeking to help novice or preservice teachers to learn strategies for teaching disabled students for the first time. However, we view this as troublesome as well, since novice or preservice teachers may simply adopt disseminated pedagogical strategies that may *appear* effective, because they were published in academic texts or journals, or because of the social capital or notoriety of the authors. Indeed, the dissemination of practices that ignore both empiricism and, more specifically, the experiences of disabled students, can lead to instances where teachers are adopting pedagogical strategies that are either ineffective or, perhaps, unintentionally harmful. More directly, we argue that the dissemination and subsequent adoption of pedagogical strategies that are (dis)connected to research may unintentionally contribute to forms of exclusion, reinforce hypermasculine and ableist cultures, and place unwanted social spotlights on disability (Slee & Allan, 2001). This to us, places onus on scholars as well as practice-based texts and journals to ensure that practices are supported by research, including those which value disabled students' voices and experiences. Or, alternatively, perhaps it is the job of scholars to note when their suggestions are *not* supported by empiricism, so that readers can make sound and logical judgments about pedagogical practices with full information at their disposal. Currently, though, there seems to be a false communication about these practices, where the (dis)connection between research and practice is hidden, and depictions of false utility are promoted.

With these considerations in mind, we suggest that the current (dis)connections that are evident in our field support the notion that teaching within integrated classes is more so about supporting the beliefs and values of adult stakeholders (e.g., teachers, higher education scholars) and less so about the experiences of disabled students. That is, we believe that the chapters in this text demonstrate that disabled students are largely exposed to classes that may be labelled as being *inclusive*, where they are expected to assimilate (Maher, 2017) into classes and experience pedagogical practices that are (dis)connected from empirical research and instead *tick a box* to communicate the appearance of meaningful and *inclusive* education (Fitzgerald & Stride, 2012). Elsewhere (Haegele & Maher, 2021), we've offered the term *inclusion porn*, encouraged by the concept of inspiration porn popularised by Stella Young, to describe instances like this where disabled people are subjected to heterogeneous spaces without deep consideration for their needs so that nondisabled stakeholders can celebrate or be satisfied with their existence within these spaces. With that, we encourage physical educators and scholars, as others have (Penney et al., 2018), who are reviewing this text to critically consider whether the pedagogical practices they adopt (or promote) are simply paying lip-service to *inclusion* so that they can become personally satisfied with their *moral* disposition towards integrated spaces, or if they have thoroughly considered empirical work, and specifically that which centres disabled voices, when constructing courses, classes and education. This message is expounded upon herein.

What Now?

We set out in this book to advocate for schools to be (more) research engaged and for physical education teachers to develop (more) research-informed practices. Thus, we encourage physical education teachers especially to carefully consider what we have found and said about the evidence supporting (or not) the practices that are most often used when teaching disabled students. According to Burn and Mutton (2015), it is crucial that teachers are able and actively endeavour to gain insights from and draw upon educational research most closely aligned to their context-bound practice to make informed decisions about curriculum, pedagogy and assessment because it can impact positively on student outcomes. In this respect, it is important that physical education teachers can evaluate research findings so they can engage in well-informed, focused, pedagogical experimentation wherein the learning and development of disabled students is carefully considered, monitored and reviewed. We return to the words of Brown (2018) whose articulation aligns with our line of thinking:

> I firmly believe that educationalists engaging with evidence is socially beneficial. This is because policy decisions or teaching practice grounded in an understanding of what is or could be effective, or even simply an understanding of what is currently known, are likely to be more successful than those based on experience or intuition alone.
>
> (p. 1)

For teachers to be able to source, understand and apply research findings to inform practice, they need support that this book cannot offer. In Chapter 2, we suggest that the development of research knowledge, skills and experiences needs to be integral to initial teacher education and continuing professional development. Initial teacher education can create an expectation among pre-service teachers that their practice should, wherever possible, be research informed. At the same time, initial teacher education can be used to develop the knowledge, skills, experience and confidence required to interpret and use research in a way suitable to the contextual needs of teachers, something we know teachers struggle to do (Coldwell et al., 2017). To help pre-service teachers to make more evidence-informed decisions when supporting disabled students in physical education, teacher educators need to ensure that:

- their curriculums include research methods training that involves gathering data with, from and/or about disabled students;
- pre-service teachers complete a research project that focuses on disabled students in physical education;
- practical activities relate to evidence-supported strategies for teaching disabled students, and that these are supported by opportunities for pre-service teachers to critically reflect on and discuss how research relating to disabled students can be used to influence the planning and teaching of practical activities; and
- relationships are developed with research engaged schools, and that professional tutors and mentors provide time and space for pre-service teachers to critical reflect on, discuss and put into practice research and theory relating to teaching disabled students in physical education.

Similar can be said about teacher continuing professional learning and development in that there is a need to provide in-service teachers with opportunities to learn about how to source, interpret and apply research findings, and to plan for, gather and analyse their own data relating to their practice. At present, there are very few professional development opportunities available to teachers to become more research engaged despite notable evidence suggesting that it can impact positively on student achievement and outcomes (see Burn & Mutton, 2015).

We know that we ask a lot. Nonetheless, we consider this a crucial direction of travel if we are to properly prepare pre- and in-service teachers for teaching disabled students, and thus improve the educational experiences and outcomes of disabled students. For this ambition to be realised, there needs to be buy in from school leaders. Indeed, in the most highly research-engaged schools, senior leaders played a key role, acting as intermediaries and facilitators of access to, engagement with and use of research evidence for staff in their schools (Coldwell et al., 2017). According to research, senior leaders in school need to be committed to cultivating a research culture in schools that includes having a strategic plan focusing on shifting school policies and practices towards a school learning culture committed to research informed school improvement where staff work collaboratively and share a commitment to understanding what works, how, when and why (Godfrey, 2016; Greany, 2015). Researchers like us have a part to play here too as knowledge creators because research suggests that schools that are most research engaged are those that are directly linked to knowledge producers (Coldwell et al., 2017). Therefore, we encourage researchers, like us, to leave behind the comforts of our ivory towers and develop productive and mutually beneficial relationships with schools to support them and their staff to connect research and practice for the benefit of the students that we all ultimately serve.

References

Alves, M. L., Haegele, J. A., & Duarte, E. (2018). "We can't do anything": The experiences of students with visual impairments in physical education classes in Brazil. *British Journal of Visual Impairment, 36*(2), 152–162. https://doi.org/10.1177%2F0264619617752761

Brown, C. (2018). *Achieving evidence-informed policy and practice in education: Evidenced.* Emerald Publishing.

Burn, K., & Mutton, T. (2015). A review of 'research-informed clinical practice' in initial teacher education. *Oxford Review of Education, 41*(2), 217–233. https://doi.org/10.1080/03054985.2015.1020104

Carter, B., Grey, J., McWilliams, E., Clair, Z., Blake, K., & Byatt, R. (2014). 'Just kids playing sport (in a chair)': Experiences of children, families and stakeholders attending a wheelchair sports club. *Disability & Society, 29*(6), 938–952. https://doi.org/10.1080/09687599.2014.880329

Coates, J. (2011). Physically fit or physically literate? How children with special educational needs understand physical education. *European Physical Education Review, 17*(2), 167–181. https://doi.org/10.1177/1356336X11413183

Coldwell, M., Greany, T., Higgins, St., Brown, C., Bronwen, M., Stiell, B., Stoll, L., Willis., B., & Burns, H. (2017). *Evidence-informed teaching: an evaluation of progress in England: Research report.* DfE.

De Kegel, A., Dhooge, I., Cambier, D., Baetens, T., Palmans, T., & Van Waelvelde, H. (2011). Test–retest reliability of the assessment of postural stability in typically developing children and in hearing impaired children. *Gait & Posture, 33*(4), 679–685. https://doi.org/10.1016/j.gaitpost.2011.02.024

Elias, N. (1978). *What is sociology?* Columbia University Press.

Fitzgerald, H. (2005). Still feeling like a spare piece of luggage? Embodied experiences of (dis)ability in physical education and school sport. *Physical Education & Sport Pedagogy, 10*(1), 41–59. https://doi.org/10.1080/1740898042000334908

Fitzgerald, H. (2012). 'Drawing' on disabled students' experiences of physical education and stakeholder responses. *Sport, Education, & Society, 17,* 443–462. https://doi.org/10.1080/13573322.2011.609290

Fitzgerald, H., & Stride, A. (2012). Stories about physical education from young people with disabilities. *International Journal of Disability, Development, & Education, 59*(3), 283–293. https://doi.org/10.1080/1034912X.2012.697743

Flintoff, A., & Fitzgerald, H. (2012). Theorizing difference and (in)equality in physical education, youth sport, and health. In F. Dowling, H. Fitzgerald, & A. Flintoff (Eds.), *Equity and difference in physical education, youth sport, and health: A narrative approach* (pp. 11–36). Routledge.

Godfrey, D. (2016). Leadership of schools as research-led organizations in the English educational environment: Cultivating a research engaged school culture. *Educational Management Administration & Leadership, 44*(2), 301–321. https://doi.org/10.1177%2F1741143213508294

Greany, T. (2015). How can evidence inform teaching and decision making across 21,000 autonomous schools? Learning from the journey in England. In C. Brown (Ed.), *Leading the use of research & evidence in schools* (pp. 11–29). IOE Press.

Grenier, M., Dyson, B., & Yeaton, P. (2005). Cooperative learning that includes students with disabilities. *Journal of Physical Education, Recreation, & Dance, 76*(6), 29–35. https://doi.org/10.1080/07303084.2005.10608264

Grenier, M., & Yeaton, P. (2019). Social thinking skills and cooperative learning for students with autism. *Journal of Physical Education, Recreation, & Dance, 90*(3), 18–21. http://doi.org/10.1080/07303084.2019.1559675

Haegele, J. A., Kirk, T. N., Holland, S. K., & Zhu, X. (2021). 'The rest of the time I would just stand there and look stupid': Access in integrated physical education among adults with visual impairments. *Sport, Education & Society, 26*(8), 862–874. https://doi.org/10.1080/13573322.2020.1805425

Haegele, J. A., & Maher, A. J. (2021). A creative nonfiction account of autistic youth experiences of integrated physical education. *Disability and Society* [online first]. https://doi.org/10.1080/09687599.2021.2007361

Haegele, J. A., & Maher, A. J. (2022). Autistic youth experiences of inclusion and feelings of belonging in integrated physical education. *Autism, 26*(1), 51–61. https://doi.org/10.1177/13623613211018637

Haegele, J. A., Sato, T., Zhu, X., & Kirk, T. N. (2019). Paraeducator support in integrated physical education as reflected by adults with visual impairments. *Adapted Physical Activity Quarterly, 36*(1), 91–108. https://doi.org/10.1123/apaq.2018-0063

Haegele, J. A., & Zhu, X. (2017). Experiences of individuals with visual impairments in integrated physical education: A retrospective study. *Research Quarterly for Exercise and Sport, 88*(4), 425–435. https://doi.org/10.1080/02701367.2017.1346781

Haegele, J. A., & Zhu, X. (2021). School-based physical education. In J. A. Haegele (Ed.), *Movement and visual impairment: Research across disciplines* (pp. 47–59). Routledge.

Harvey, W. J., Wilkinson, S., Presse, C., Joober, R., & Grizenko, N. (2014). Children say the darndest things: Physical activity and children with attention-deficit hyperactivity disorder. *Physical Education & Sport Pedagogy, 19*(2), 205–220. https://doi.org/10.1080/17408989.2012.754000

Healy, S., Aigner, C., & Haegele, J. A. (2019). Prevalence of overweight and obesity among US youth with autism spectrum disorder. *Autism, 23*(4), 1046e1050. https://doi.org/10.1177%2F1362361318791817

Healy, S., Haegele, J. A., Grenier, M., & Garcia, J. M. (2017). Physical activity, screen-time behavior, and obesity among 13-year olds in Ireland with and without autism spectrum disorder. *Journal of Autism & Developmental Disorders, 47*, 49–57. https://doi.org/10.1007/s10803-016-2920-4

Hodge, S. R., Lieberman, L. J., & Murata, N. M. (2012). *Essentials of teaching adapted physical education: Diversity, culture, and inclusion.* Routledge.

Holland, K., & Haegele, J. A. (2021). Perspectives of students with disabilities toward physical education: A review update 2014–2019. *Kinesiology Review, 10*(1), 78–87. https://doi.org/10.1123/kr.2020-0002

King-Sears, M. (2020). Introduction to special series on universal design for learning. *Remedial and Special Education, 41*(4), 191–193. https://doi.org/10.1177%2F0741932520908342

Li, C., Haegele, J., & Wu, L. (2018). Comparing physical activity and sedentary behavior levels between deaf and hearing adolescents. *Disability and Health Journal, 12*(3), 514–518. https://doi.org/10.1016/j.dhjo.2018.12.002

Lieberman, L. J., & Houston-Wilson, C. (2018). *Strategies for inclusion: Physical education for all* (3rd ed.). Human Kinetics.

Lobenius-Palmér, K., Sjqvist, B., Hurtig-Wennlof, A., & Lundqvist, L. (2018). Accelerometer-assessed physical activity and sedentary time in youth with disabilities. *Adapted Physical Activity Quarterly, 35,* 1–19. https://doi.org/10.1123/apaq.2015-0065

Maher, A. (2017). "We've got a few who don't go to PE": Learning support assistant and special educational needs coordinators views on inclusion in physical education in England. *European Physical Education Review, 23*(2), 257–270. https://doi.org/10.1177%2F1356336X16649938

Majlesi, M., Farahpour, N., Azadian, E., & Amini, M. (2014). The effect of interventional proprioceptive training on static balance and gait in deaf children. *Research in Developmental Disabilities, 35*(12), 3562–3567. https://doi.org/10.1016/j.ridd.2014.09.001

Martin Ginis, K. A., Evans, M. B., Mortenson, W. B., & Noreau, L. (2017). Broadening the conceptualization of participation of persons with physical educations: A configurative review and recommendations. *Archives of Physical Medicine & Rehabilitation, 98*(2), 395–402.

Morley, D., Banks, T., Haslingden, C., Kirk, B., Parkinson, S., van Rossum, T., Morley, I., & Maher, A. (2021). Including pupils with special educational needs and/or disabilities in mainstream secondary physical education: A revisit study. *European Physical Education Review, 27*(2), 401–418. https://doi.org/10.1177/1356336X20953872

Ok, M.-W., Rao, K., Bryant, B., & McDougall, D. (2017). Universal design for learning in Pre-K to grade 12 classrooms: A systematic review of research. *Exceptionality, 25*(2), 116–138. https://doi.org/10.1080/09362835.2016.1196450

Penney, D., Jeanes, R., O'Connor, J., & Alfrey, L. (2018). Re-theorising inclusion and reframing inclusive practice in physical education. *International Journal of Inclusive Education, 22*(10), 1062–1077. https://doi.org/10.1080/13603116.2017.1414888

Reich, W. (2010). Three problems of intersubjectivity—and one solution. *Sociological Theory, 28*(1), 41–63. https://doi.org/10.1111%2Fj.1467-9558.2009.01364.x

Rine, R., Cornwall, G., Can, K., Locascio, C., O'hare, T., Robinson, E., & Rice, M. (2000). Evidence of progressive delay of motor development in children with sensorineural hearing loss and concurrent vestibular dysfunction. *Perceptual and Motor Skills, 90*(3), 1101–1112. https://doi.org/10.2466%2Fpms.2000.90.3c.1101

Shields, N., Synnot, A., & Barr, M. (2012). Perceived barriers and facilitators to physical activity for children with disability: A systematic review. *British Journal of Sports Medicine, 46*(14), 989–997. http://doi.org/10.1136/bjsports-2011-090236

Slee, R., & Allan, J. (2001). Excluding the included: A recognition of inclusive education. *International Studies in Sociology of Education, 11*92), 173–192. https://doi.org/10.1080/09620210100200073

Vickerman, P., & Maher, A. (2018) *Teaching physical education to pupils with special educational needs and disabilities* (2nd ed.). Sage.

Winnick, J. P., & Porretta, D. L. (2017). *Adapted physical education and sports* (6th ed.). Human Kinetics.

Index

9 781032 008950